Meg Cabot is the author of many books for young adults, including the *The Princess Diaries* series, *All American Girl*, *Teen Idol*, *Nicola and the Viscount* and *Victoria and the Rogue*, as well as several books for adult readers. Meg lives in Florida with her husband and one-eyed cat, Henrietta, and says she is still waiting for her real parents, the king and queen, to restore her to her rightful throne.

There are two Walt Disney films based on *The Princess Diaries*.

Visit Meg Cabot's website at
www.megcabot.co.uk

Items should be returned on or before the last date shown below. Items not already requested by other borrowers may be renewed in person, in writing or by telephone. To renew, please quote the number on the barcode label. To renew online a PIN is required. This can be requested at your local library.
Renew online @ **www.dublincitypubliclibraries.ie**
Fines charged for overdue items will include postage incurred in recovery. Damage to or loss of items will be charged to the borrower.

First published 2005 by Macmillan Children's Books
a division of Macmillan Publishers Limited
20 New Wharf Road, London N1 9RR
Basingstoke and Oxford
www.panmacmillan.com

Associated companies throughout the world

ISBN 0 330 43505 1

1 3 5 7 9 8 6 4 2

A CIP catalogue record for this book is available from
the British Library.

Printed and bound in China.

For all the holiday princesses (and princes) out there

CONTENTS

local renown, sheds light on holiday practices ancient and obscure, and Frank Gianini, algebra teacher, reveals a practice druidic in nature

- *Egg-balancing, leather bikinis, wassail and faux mistletoe*

V. Christmas Around the World

Lilly Moscovitz in New York City, Dowager Princess Clarisse Renaldo in Genovia, Hank Thermopolis in Versailles, Indiana, and Princess Mia all around the world

- *Plus the top ten holiday movies, annotated by Lilly and Mia*

VI. Xmas Xtras

Princess Mia's grandmother, mother, father and two schoolmates illuminate various Christmas traditions

- *The debunking of Santa Claus, the Christmas star and Good King Wenceslas. Also, Christmas trees of artistic merit and pop-culture interest and royal advent calendars*

VII. Celebrating Kwanzaa

Shameeka Taylor, Albert Einstein High School cheerleader, on the yearly tradition of African-American pride and commemoration.

- *Also: a fun cheer to perform in solidarity and while you're waiting for the benne cakes to bake*

VIII. Happy New Year!

Tina Hakim Baba, romance specialist, on the all-important New Year's Kiss, musical genius Boris Pelkowski on 'Auld Lang Syne', and more

- *Plus how to say 'Happy New Year!' the world over*

IX. Chinese New Year

Princess Mia interviews Ling Su Wong, friend, artist and Chinese American

- *Ling Su explains it all to Mia, and dishes about Chinese astrology*

X. Conclusion

Are you listening?

- *Pass the gifts, please*

Mia's Christmas

I. Introduction

Sleigh Bells Ring

A Note from Her Royal Highness Princess Amelia Mignonette Grimaldi Thermopolis Renaldo

Sleigh bells ring! Are you listening? In the lane, snow is glistening . . .

Well, OK, whatever, I've never actually heard sleigh bells. And there are no lanes in New York City, just streets and avenues (unless you count Minetta Lane down in the Village, which I don't because it smells like pee), and the snow never glistens here – it turns almost instantly into black slush because of all the car exhaust.

But that doesn't mean I don't wholeheartedly enjoy the holiday season when I get the chance. There's so much to do and see, sometimes I wonder how I'll ever get to it all.

That's why I, with the assistance of some of my friends and relatives, have composed this guide, to help make what often turns out to be a hectic and stressful time more relaxed, so that we can all actually take the time to enjoy it. Because that's what the holiday season is all about – enjoying time with friends and family!

II. Holiday Etiquette

A Note from Her Royal Highness
Princess Mia Thermopolis

The holidays aren't just any other days . . . well, duh, since they're called holidays. But you get what I mean. They come laden with all this . . . stuff. Like, traditions.

And while some people, like my mom, believe traditions are for breaking, some other people, like Grandmere, believe traditions are, like, the backbone of the family and society and stuff.

I don't know who's right and who's wrong. Maybe they both are. All I know is, none of this has anything to do with presents. Which is a bummer, if you ask me.

HOLIDAY CARDS
Sending Joy to Your Loved Ones for the Price of a Stamp

By Clarisse Marie Grimaldi Renaldo, Dowager Princess of Genovia and Grandmere of the Princess Mia Thermopolis [with commentary by the Princess herself]

Cards sent during the holiday season are a lovely way to say *Joyeux Noël*, Happy Hanukkah or *Bonne*

Année to a friend or family member with whom you are not necessarily close enough to exchange gifts, but whom you nonetheless wish to acknowledge.

The first Christmas card was sent by Sir Henry Cole, an Englishman who, in 1843, wished to urge his friends not to forget the needy during the holiday season. He commissioned a small illustration of a happy family enjoying a succulent meal while failing to notice the destitute and squalid conditions of the poor around them, and sent it to all of his acquaintances.

I totally applaud Sir Henry for the thought, but bummer card to get in the mail!

The tradition Sir Henry began soon caught on, and sending illustrated cards at Christmas became the rage. It is now a billion-dollar-a-year industry worldwide. It has grown so widespread, in fact, with people sending so many cards to so many people,

that they have managed to forget basic card etiquette: a card, however beautifully rendered, is not as important as the message written inside it. And by that I do not mean the message the card manufacturer has printed inside it but the message YOU, the SENDER, has written inside it.

Because the recipient of your card does not particularly care if Hallmark wishes him or her a Happy New Year. What the recipient of your card cares about is YOU, and how YOU are doing.

That is why it is essential to HANDWRITE a short note in each and every card you send, no matter how many cards that may be. The Palais Royale du Genovia sends out over one thousand cards per year, and I personally handwrite a message in each one, such as:

Dearest Charles,

I do hope you and Camilla will drop in during your next trip to Biarritz.

   Merry Christmas, and the happiest of New Years to you and your children.

Much love,

Clarisse

This is perfectly adequate. It is, of course, ultimately the thought that counts.

   This does not mean, however, that the horrid American tradition of sending photocopied 'Christmas newsletters' is acceptable! Far from it. I can understand persons with children wishing to let friends and family know of their progeny's progress in school or games. And therefore I will allow that a one-page note of this kind, WITH A PERSONAL MESSAGE HANDWRITTEN ACROSS THE TOP, ENCLOSED IN A TASTEFUL CARD, is permissible.

What I cannot condone are the two-, three-, or even FOUR-page single-spaced NOVELS people seem to feel compelled to send today. I do not particularly care to know the details of 'Grandmums' latest knee surgery, or the final score of every single one of 'Harry's' polo matches. Careful selection of the year's highlights, related in a fairly HUMOROUS manner, is the only way letters of this kind can succeed.

Since it seems highly unlikely, however, that anyone is ever going to follow my advice, I can only hope the holiday newsletter goes the way of bell-bottoms and fades from view.

Uh, Grandmere? Bell-bottoms are back in style now. And I personally LOVE getting Christmas newsletters, the longer the better. My favourite is the one Mr Gianini's sister sends out every year listing her kids' — Nathan and Claire — many social and athletic accomplishments. For instance, Nathan was voted Heaviest Sleeper at his sleepaway camp last summer. And Claire graduated from the Barbizon School of Modelling with top honours, particularly in Runway Walking and Product Endorsement. It warms my heart each holiday season to know that Nathan and Claire? Yeah, they're just keepin' it real.

IT'S NOT JUST ABOUT GIFTS -
Plus Snip-n-save Gift List!
By Princess Mia Thermopolis

Everyone knows that Christmas is the celebration of the birth of Jesus Christ, who was born nearly two thousand years ago. The funny thing is, no one really knows whether Jesus was REALLY born on December 25. Probably, in fact, he wasn't, and this date was chosen because the popular ancient Persian god Mithras was also supposedly born on this day.

But who cares? It's still a totally fun holiday – especially when combined with all that Santa stuff and, of course, PRESENTS.

Some historians say we give presents at Christmas time because that's what the ancient Romans used to do at Saturnalia, a winter-solstice celebration. Others say we give presents because of the gifts the three wise men brought to baby Jesus. Still others say we give gifts in memory of St Nicholas, who was a really generous guy.

I say: who cares WHY we give gifts? Just keep 'em coming.

Oh yeah: it's important to GIVE. Otherwise, you won't RECEIVE.

Handy Snip-n-save Royal Genovian Gift List

FOR   **GIFT IDEA**

Mom: _____
                           _____
Dad: _____
                           _____
Step-parents: _____
                           _____
Siblings: _____
                           _____
                           _____
                           _____
                           _____
Best friend: _____
                           _____
                           _____

Other friends: _____

_____

_____

_____

_____

_____

Boyfriend: _____

Grandparents: _____

_____

Uncles, aunts, _____
cousins:

_____

_____

Pet: _____

Biology lab partner: _____

Teachers: _____

_____

Postal carrier: _____

Newspaper deliverer: _____

Favourite Chinese-
food delivery person: _____

Bodyguard: _____

Royal chauffeur: _____

Personal maid: _____

Others: _____

_____

_____

_____

GIFTS FOR GUYS
Just Say No to Expensive Electronics
By Tina Hakim Baba, Romance Expert
[with commentary by Princess Mia Thermopolis]

Let's face it. Guys are IMPOSSIBLE to shop for.
The only person harder to shop for than your dad is
your boyfriend, and that's because your boyfriend's

gift has to be imbued with all this meaning and stuff. Otherwise, it's, like, what's the point?

Hopefully you and your guy have some private jokes or at least shared musical taste. That way you can always get him a joke present – like, if you two are obsessed with the violinist Joshua Bell, you could get him an autographed 8 x 11 of Joshua Bell – or a CD he's been dying to hear.

But let's say your private jokes are about something that can't be bought in a store, purchased from a fan club, or even handmade, and a CD just won't cut it. What's a lovelorn girl to do?

Follow these simple steps, and the hearth glow of your love will never die.

Gifts for the Guy You Aren't Dating, but Hope to Some Day

FOOD. The way to a man (or woman's) heart is through the stomach. You can never go wrong with gifts of homemade cookies, candy or fudge (homemade cheese balls make excellent gifts for people on a low-carb or sugar-free diet). Just make sure your guy doesn't have any food allergies – if he does, do not prepare him something containing that substance.

Food gifts are appropriate for ANY guy of ANY duration of acquaintance. They are ALWAYS welcome. Whether it's the hot guy who works out next to you at the gym, your lab partner or just the cute guy you see sometimes at the bus stop, just fork over a prettily wrapped tin of whatever, say, 'I made this for you. Happy holidays!' and he'll be blushing to his hairline.

To avoid teasing/rumours, you might want to give similarly wrapped tins to friends, so he doesn't think he's the ONLY one who got one and that you're a creepy stalker he should run from like a startled fawn.

Gifts for the Guy You've Been Out with Only Once or Twice on Group Dates

Food is an excellent gift for this person too, but you could move up a smidge on the intimacy scale and give him something else handmade, such as mittens if you knit, or a CD mix you burned yourself. A book or DVD might also be appropriate. Expensive jewellery or clothing is NOT acceptable for this person. He hasn't professed his undying love for you and so does not deserve to be showered with electronics or gold at this point in the relationship.

Gifts for the Guy You're Dating Exclusively

This is the hardest person of all to shop for – or the easiest, depending. Again, gifts based on private jokes are always good. Food is good, but remember, he isn't going to gaze at an empty tin when he thinks of you the way he would the stunning portrait you had your little brother take with your iCamera and had framed in a beautiful homemade frame.

Whatever you do, do NOT spend an exorbitant sum on a gift for your romantic partner. Christmas, Hanukkah and Kwanzaa gifts are supposed to be MEANINGFUL, not expensive. Do NOT, for instance, buy him a gold ID bracelet because you're hoping he'll ask YOU to wear it. Do not buy him a leather jacket for the same reason, or a CD player (so NOT meaningful) or car stereo. You want to make sure he's staying with you for YOU, not your money.

This is why the best gift for your one true love is ALWAYS a kiss accompanied by something you made yourself, be it food, a CD or a lovely hand-knitted steering-wheel cover.

I could not agree more.

Truer words were never spoken. I tried out my Christmas-Ornaments-As-Earrings Scheme and it went over like a charm. Until Principal Gupta saw them and made me take them out. Who knew Rudolph and Frosty weren't part of Albert Einstein High's regulation school uniform?

Princess Party Tip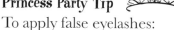

To apply false eyelashes:

+ First, make up your eyes in your normal fashion (shadow, liner, mascara). You will have a hard time applying these things AFTER the lashes are glued on.

+ Next, TRIM the lashes to fit the width of your eyes. False eyelashes are NOT one size fits all.

+ Then apply a SMALL amount of the glue that came with the lashes (remember, you are putting glue NEAR YOUR EYE. USE ONLY SPECIALLY DESIGNED FALSE-EYELASH GLUE FOR THIS) and, with tweezers or clean fingers, apply lashes to the upper lid, making sure to tamp them down so that they rest against your real eyelashes.

- Don't expect to execute the above move in one try. It will take LOTS of practice before you get it right. ·

- Once you've gotten it right, and after the glue has dried, gently CURL your lashes with your eyelash curler so the fake ones blend better with your real lashes, then apply another layer of mascara. Blink a few times to make sure the fake lashes stay in place.

- You're good to go!

Enjoy!

HOLIDAY GIFT WRAP
You CAN Judge a Gift by Its Cover
By Sebastiano, Royal Fashion Designer
and Wardrobe Consultant
[with commentary by Princess Mia Thermopolis]

You do not need to spend a fort* this hol* seas* on exp* gift-wrap* paper! You can make your own! Is EASY! Just fol* these sim* steps!

Sebastiano still has trouble grasping basic English, as it is a second language for him. What he means is, You don't need to spend a fortune this holiday season on expensive gift-wrapping paper. Just follow these simple steps — Here, why don't I just translate the rest.

You will need:

+ butcher paper (available in any art store)[1]
+ scissors
+ acrylic paint
+ paintbrushes
+ tape

Cut out the desired amount of butcher paper needed to cover the gift. Using the acrylic paint and your imagination, paint colourful designs or messages all over one side of the paper (important: paint just ONE side of the paper). After the paint is fully dry, wrap your present, using tape to hold the paper in place.

[1] You can also use newspaper pages torn from magazines for a more colourful or collage-y effect.

Beautiful and personal!

You may want to use raffia (available at any plant store) as ribbon.

See? Beaut*!

Beautiful.

III. Hanukkah Lights

A Note from Her Royal Highness Princess Mia Thermopolis

Hanukkah, or the Feast of the Dedication, is an ancient Jewish celebration, in which everyone gets a lot more presents than I do, which is not fair.

Also, everyone gets to eat latkes, which are potato pancakes that you dip in sour cream . . . not to be confused with scallion pancakes from Number One Noodle Son, which you dip in soy sauce. But just as tasty, actually.

GO TEAM MACCABEE

By Michael Moscovitz,
Royal Consort to the Princess of Genovia
[with commentary by the Princess herself]

Contrary to popular opinion, Hanukkah isn't about getting eight presents on eight consecutive nights. Well, I mean, that happens. But that's not what it's about.

Hanukkah is actually a celebration dating back to two thousand years ago, in Palestine, when Antiochus the Syrian, a guy who hated everybody and vowed to destroy all faiths but his own, was killed by the Maccabees led by Judas (no, not the same one from the Mel Gibson movie).

Everyone was psyched Antiochus was finally dead, and ready to get back to their normal routine. But when they went to light the eternal flame in the Temple lamp, there was only a small container of sacred oil left – just about enough for a single night, which was a huge deal, because in order to reconsecrate the Temple, which Antiochus had basically trashed, they had to have the eternal flame going . . . and it was going to take eight days to fetch new oil.

Which meant, basically, that Judas was screwed.

So you can imagine his surprise – not to mention everyone else's – when that one little container of oil miraculously lasted throughout the eight days it took to get more oil. It's this miracle that Jews celebrate during the eight nights of Hanukkah, when we gather in our homes to light the eight candles in the Hanukkah lamp.

Don't forget the presents.

Traditionally, on the eight nights of Hanukkah, children are given gifts.

Eight gifts. One for every night. Which is way more than I ever get at Christmas.
Not that it's about the gifts, of course.

One of the best-known symbols of Hanukkah is the dreidel. Although the dreidel (the origins of which go back to a game called 'totum' or 'teetotum', which was played in England and Ireland in the sixteenth century) has long been associated with Hanukkah and children, the story behind the dreidel is actually super serious: in times when Jews were forbidden to meet and practise their religious beliefs, men would keep a dreidel and gelt (money) handy while gathering to study the Torah (the Hebrew Bible). Whenever soldiers approached, the men would pull out the dreidel and pretend to be playing a game. So, basically, the dreidel saved their lives.

And this is where we get the famous dreidel song:

Dreidel dreidel dreidel
I made it out of clay
And when it's dry and ready
Then dreidel I will play

Not to be confused with the other famous Hanukkah song by Adam Sandler.

Princess Party Tip

Forget spin the bottle! At your next party, play spin the dreidel! Players can use coins, candy, nuts, raisins or chocolate coins (gelt) as tokens or chips. Each player spins the dreidel in turn. When the dreidel stops, the letter that is facing up decides the player's fate:

נ – nothing happens: next player spins the dreidel

ג – player takes all tokens in the pot

ה – player takes half of the pot

ש – player must put one token into the pot.

(Together these letters stand for *Nes Gadol Haya Sham*, which means, 'A Great Miracle Happened There.' In Israel the dreidel is a bit different, with letters that mean, 'A Great Miracle Happened HERE.')

You can also play the dreidel MY way: whoever the dreidel points at when it stops is the person the spinner has to kiss.

Enjoy!

IV. Yuletide Past and Present

A Note from Her Royal Highness Princess Mia Thermopolis

Did you ever wonder where all the crazy holiday traditions come from? My mom says they all come from Mamaw, her mother back in Versailles, Indiana, and that's why we must rebel against them with all our might.

But my mom's not actually right about that – the Mamaw part, I mean. Most of the holiday traditions we participate in today actually got their start way, way before Mamaw was ever born.

Although you might not believe it, to look at her.

Mamaw, I mean. Especially when she's not wearing her bridge.

A BRIEF HISTORY OF THE SOLSTICE - OUR PAGAN PAST

*By Lilly Moscovitz, Creator, Writer, Director
and Host of 'Lilly Tells It Like It Is'
[with commentary by Princess Mia Thermopolis]*

So, let's face it: winter sucks.

Oh, sure, there's the ice skating and hot chocolate and the Non-Denominational Winter Dance and stuff.

But there didn't used to be. A long time ago, back in what they call pagan times, before they had mini-marshmallows or Times Square or even electricity, people used to get really bummed out around December 21. That's because December 21 was (and still is) the shortest day of the year, also known as the winter solstice (when the sun is at its greatest distance from the celestial equator, which means as far as it gets from the earth).

On the solstice, you can supposedly balance an egg on its head and it will stay like that. Because of the magnetic forces. Try it, it works ... if you practise enough.

Anyway, for ancient people who worshipped the

sun and all that, the winter solstice truly sucked, because they feared that the gods had forsaken them, since the days were getting shorter.

You would think, considering this happened EVERY year, they'd have caught on sooner or later. But whatever.

They got all scared life on earth as they knew it would end if the gods didn't let the sun shine again.

So the ancients did what any of us would do when we're feeling bummed.

They partied.

Seriously. They built these big fires to encourage the sun to shine again, and then, when it worked (because, um, it always worked), they'd party with these giant feasts and stuff, because they all realized spring was coming and they weren't all going to die after all.

Some of these ancient parties included:

- Feast of Aset – the Egyptians, who were big partiers, held a winter festival that honoured Isis (Aset), mother of the sky god, Horus. It probably wasn't a good idea to be around during the Feast of Aset if you were a virgin. Or a sheep.

- Saturnalia – the Romans paid homage to Saturn, the god of agriculture, with this festival. People pranced around with garlands on their heads, giving candles and green wreaths as presents. And, knowing the ancient Romans, there was probably some throwing up as well.

- Feast of Mithras – to the Persians (where Iran is today) December 25 was Unconquered Sun (Mithras) Day. They were so successful in promoting this belief that it even spread to ancient Britain, until King Arthur was all, ENOUGH already, and ran around cutting off people's heads with the help of Keira Knightley in her leather bikini.

✦ Yule – the Norsemen started this big feast called 'Jiuleis' or 'Giuli', later shortened to just plain 'Yule'. Beginning on December 20 or 21, Yule spanned twelve days, ending with 'Yule Night' on December 31 (this is where the twelve days of Christmas come from. Although I highly doubt these guys messed around with any partridges, except to eat them). These dudes would kill a bunch of cows when the grasses died out and roast them over a yule log, which was lit from a piece of the previous year's yule log that had been saved (actually, the whole Christmas-tree thing that we enjoy today is an extension of Yule, since it was thought that the sacrifice of a great tree would ensure that life would go on in spite of the cold and bad weather).

Wiccans still celebrate Yule as the first of the solar festivals and the first sabbath of the new year, doing stuff like carolling and wassailing.

I love 'Charmed' even though they've never actually shown Alyssa Milano wassailing. I would love it even more if they WOULD show this.

However these ancient midwinter feasts and festivals were carried out – from Mithras to Saturnalia – they all had one thing in common: they were parties to celebrate the victory of light and life over darkness, and a time of hope born anew.

Also the time for the getting of presents. Such as the Segway Human Transporter I've been wanting for a VERY long time.

Princess Party Tip

You can have your own little Wiccan Yule celebration by simmering the following on a stove:

+ 1 gallon sparkling apple juice

- 25 – 30 whole cloves
- 6 – 10 cinnamon sticks
- 1 quart pineapple juice
- 16 oz can frozen orange-juice concentrate

Serves 8–10

Sounds a lot like hot fizzy apple juice, doesn't it? Well, it's not. It's wassail!
    Enjoy!

HOLLY AND MISTLETOE
Druid's Delite

By Frank Gianini, Algebra Teacher and
Stepfather of Princess Mia Thermopolis
[with commentary by the Princess herself]

OK, so holly comes from this bush, see, and was traditionally the sacred plant of Saturn, and so it was very popular at the ancient Roman Saturnalia festival around solstice time (December 21), where everybody traditionally got down and drank a lot. Like a Grateful Dead concert, only no Jerry Garcia. Romans used to give one another holly wreaths during Saturnalia to decorate the house with – kind of the way Deadheads do with tie-dyed stuff.

A bunch of centuries later, in December, while the Romans continued doing their pagan thing, Christians celebrated the birth of Jesus. Only to avoid getting found out (you know, that they weren't into Saturn like everybody else) they decorated their homes with Saturnalia holly.

Just like the song 'Ring a Ring of Roses' turns out to be about the plague, the song 'Deck the Halls with Boughs of

Holly' is actually about avoiding religious persecution through subterfuge. Who knew?

As there got to be more and more Christians, and their customs became more popular, holly lost its pagan association and became a symbol of Christmas. Get it?

And mistletoe. OK, mistletoe is basically a weed that has no roots of its own. Instead, it lives off the tree that it attaches itself to, like a leech. Or like Yoko Ono, you know, when she attached herself to the Beatles.

Still, in ancient times, mistletoe was thought to have these miraculous heal-ing properties (like another weed we all know), as well as bringing good luck to who-ever stood under a sprig of it.

Eventually this evolved to whoever stood under it getting kissed by whoever was standing nearby.

Princess Party Tip

Real mistletoe in short supply? Make your own! All you need is:

+ green felt
+ white imitation pearls
+ scissors
+ glue

Cut two leaf shapes out of the green felt. Glue them together. In the middle of where they are joined, glue several imitation pearls. Let dry. Then hold your fake mistletoe over your head when a cute guy approaches and tell him he has to kiss you.

It works!

Enjoy!

v. Christmas Around the World

A Note from Her Royal Highness Princess Mia Thermopolis

It's easy to think, when you're caught up in the holiday hordes on the subway, trying to get home after a brutal day at the Tiffany's gift counter – where all you wanted to buy was a crystal apple for your French teacher, Mademoiselle Klein, but this lady from New Jersey who was buying a key chain shaped like a golf bag kept cutting in front of you until finally you had to be all, 'LADY! I WAS HERE FIRST!' – that this is what Christmas is like around the world: the snow, the angry taxi drivers, the tourists asking you where they can find Green-Witch Village . . .

But the truth is, Christmas is celebrated in VERY different ways outside of New York . . . and even outside of America. Who knew that not everyone watches the burning yule log on Channel Eleven Christmas morning?

Not me.

CHRISTMAS IN NYC
TV and Chinese Food, Baby
By Lilly Moscovitz, Independent Christmas Observer

Even though I am Jewish I can tell you all about Christmas in New York. In fact, I am probably in a BETTER position to tell you about Christmas in New York than anyone, as I am unbiased towards the season and more of an independent observer of the whole thing.

The Christmas Season in New York City officially begins the day after Thanksgiving, also commonly referred to by the retail industry as Black Friday. This is because the day after Thanksgiving, which many New Yorkers have off, is when most people begin their Christmas shopping. It is usually the busiest shopping day of the year (followed by December 26, on which everyone exchanges the things people bought the day after Thanksgiving).

It is around this time that department stores in New York City unveil their Christmas window displays. Many New Yorkers – not to mention tourists visiting the city – take an afternoon to walk around and admire these displays, which can contain animatronic puppets, music (actually piped outside through loudspeakers) and even live actors, though sadly none you'd actually want to see. Generally these displays are reviewed in the newspaper, and those declared most creative become the most popular and are a source of pride for the store.

On December 1 or thereabouts, a giant tree is put up in Rockefeller Center (next to the big gold man statue who guards the ice-skating rink). A committee is formed every year to scour the country for the biggest, nicest tree in the land, and then whoever owns it is asked to donate it to the city. Usually people are so honoured they say yes. This is when Mia usually starts complaining about what a mean thing that is to do to a nice old tree.

Then the tree is decorated, and a few days later, in a solemn ceremony featuring performances from many fine artists (note sarcasm) like Mariah Carey or Celine Dion, the tree is lit by the mayor or some other dignitary. This indicates to New Yorkers that they have only a few weeks left to finish their Christmas shopping and throws

them into a rabid frenzy of shopaholism, so that they're in a worse mood than ever. Also around this time, the first snowfall of the year will occur, causing huge traffic headaches and making it impossible to find a parking place.

After this, it's just a matter of getting your shopping done and getting all of your Christmas supplies together before the stores sell out of them.

At the loft on Thompson Street, Mia's Christmas Eve tradition, which I observed many times, USED to include a delivery from Number One Noodle Son, tree decorating and movies.

But now that Mia is the Princess of Genovia, she has to spend Christmas at the palace over there.

But back BEFORE she became a princess, Mia and her mom (and sometimes me if I was invited, which I usually was if Hanukkah didn't happen to fall on the same day) would order cold sesame noodles, jumbo prawns in garlic sauce and sautéed string beans from their favourite Chinese takeout place, then make ornaments for their tree in the shapes of celebrities who had died the previous year. Then they'd settle in to watch *A Christmas Story* on TNT, sometimes followed by *Home for the Holidays* or *The Ref*, their other two favourite holiday movies.

Christmas morning, after sleeping in, Mia and her mom would have Christmas pancakes (pancakes in the shape of Christmas trees, an invention of Mia's mom) and open presents. Sometimes Mia's mom's friends would stop by (now Mr Gianini's parents come over, to see the baby). Mia would usually never stick around for this, though, and would instead head on over to MY apartment to show off whatever presents she'd gotten, and hope for a glimpse of my brother's naked chest as he emerged from the shower or whatever (though she doesn't know I know this. Also, GROSS).

In many parts of the country, shops and cinemas are closed on Christmas Day. Not in New York. That's because there's such a large multicultural community there – not everyone celebrates Christmas. So you can go to any restaurant, most shops and any cinemas just like on a regular day. On Christmas Day Mia used to join us on a trip to the movies and then to Chinatown for dim sum.

That is, until she became Princess of Genovia and was forced to spend all of her holidays in Genovia. Where there is no Chinatown. Or dim sum. Or snow.

I'm telling you, Christmas in New York can't be beat.

I can't believe she knew about my spying on Michael the WHOLE TIME!!!!!!!!!!!!!!!

CHRISTMAS IN GENOVIA
The Perfect Holiday

By Grandmere, Dowager Princess of Genovia
[with commentary by Princess Mia Thermopolis]

Christmas is a magical time in the small European principality of Genovia. Shopkeepers dress their windows with only the most tasteful of holiday

displays, and the sound of church bells ringing in Advent fills the ears and warms the heart.

Those stupid bells are so loud, they wake me up at the crack of dawn. I don't know how anybody is supposed to be filled with the Christmas spirit on only like five hours' sleep.

The bustling marketplace is filled with succulent treats of the season, such as figs, truffles, tangerines and smoked fish. In the patisserie, beautiful *bûches de Noël* are on display, with intricate leaves made from buttercream. And everywhere can be heard the happy cries of *'Joyeux Noel!'* from the townsfolk.

I seriously don't know what Grandmere is talking about.

All I ever hear when I go down into the marketplace is people saying, 'Get out of my way!' and 'Move!', so they can get their Christmas shopping over with and be home in time for 'Baywatch'.

Christmas Eve is, of course, one of the most exciting nights of the year in Genovia. It's when the tree in the Palais Royale is unveiled, in all of its bejewelled glory, for the first time. Champagne flows, and one can feel a frisson of festivity in the air!

I think Grandmere is mistaking the fumes from her cigarettes for frisson. That's the only thing I've ever noticed in the air on Christmas Eve.

It is Genovian tradition to eat a humble repast the night before Christmas, and so a meagre supper of lobster bisque, mussels in white-wine sauce, brandade, various salads and breads, assorted cheeses and fruits, followed by meringue, is consumed before everyone heads off to midnight Mass in the chapel. Nothing could be more beautiful than hearing the Royal Genovian Choir raise their voices in a jubilant rendition of 'Adeste Fidelis'.

'O, Come All Ye Faithful' in American.

After Mass, everyone returns to the palace and to bed, to be wakened in the morning by the joyous ringing of church bells.

Yeah. At eight in the morning. After having been at church until one. I always feel joyous about that all right.

Then everyone gathers for a delicious champagne breakfast of omelettes and beignets, while gifts brought during the night by Père Noël are opened. The happy cries of the village children as they find their Christmas dreams coming true can

be heard through the French windows, left open to let in the warm sea breeze and gentle Mediterranean sunlight.

Unless my dad has a hang-over, which he usually does. Then he makes Grandmere shut the French windows because the Mediterranean sunlight doesn't feel so gentle to HIM.

After the last gift has been unwrapped, we head to the Genovian hospital and orphanage, bearing gifts of candy and toys to those in need. Because, after all, that's what the holiday season is all about – giving to those less fortunate than yourself. God bless us, everyone!

Oh, brother!

CHRISTMAS IN INDIANA -
I Wasn't the One Who Shot That Horse

By Hank Thermopolis, Underwear Model and Hoosier

Princess Mia asked me to jaw about Christmas in my hometown of Versailles, Indiana, and I said I'd be right pleased to.

Christmas is a BIG DEAL in Versailles. First

off, Mamaw and Papaw (they raised me from a baby on account of my real mom, Mia's mom's sister, living on that commune) start putting up the Christmas decorations at the Handy Dandy Hardware Store just after Halloween. Some folks complain that they shouldn't be up before Thanksgiving, but Mamaw says they're just Christmas-hating Scrooges.

New Yorkers may think they're fancy with their big tree at Rockefeller Center, but in Versailles we got our own tradition: we string pretty lights up all around the courthouse and turn them on on December 1. You should see 'em twinkle! For a while you could take a carriage ride around the square under the lights at night, until Jim Waddell and some of his friends (I didn't have nothing to do with it, despite what some folks might believe) took to shooting at the horses with their BB guns and frighted one so bad it took off down the street. Unfortunately for Jim, the mayor and his wife and kids were inside the carriage Old Grey was pulling at the time.

After that, the mayor said no more carriage rides. Also, Jim went to jail. Old Grey was fine though, don't you worry.

Christmas Eve at Mamaw and Papaw's, it's traditional to decorate the tree (a real one Papaw and me cut down from Musgrove Orchard and tie to the roof of the car real fast before Old Man Musgrove can catch us) and drink egg-nog while listening to Mamaw's favourite Christmas record, Reba's 'Fancy' ('I may have been born just plain white trash, but Fancy was my name'). Usually everyone we know stops by for some nog, and Mamaw fries up some funnel cakes. Then we watch *Grandma Got Run Over by a Reindeer* or *Ernest Saves Christmas* and hit the hay, since Santa's on his way!

Christmas morning, we have to wake up bright and early in order to get to all those presents. We open 'em up, while Mamaw whips up some biscuits and gravy and country-fried ham. Then we change into our Sunday best and head over to church. Usually there's a Christmas pageant with real live sheep, and one of 'em almost always gets away. So me and Terry Pritchard have to spend most of the sermon chasin' it. After church, it's back home to change into civvies and head on over to the shooting range to show off whatever gun Santa brought.

And that's a real Hoosier Christmas!

I am speechless.

CHRISTMAS AROUND THE WORLD
One Crazy Night - Dozens of Ways to Celebrate It
By Princess Mia Thermopolis

Christmas is celebrated many ways throughout the world. Not everyone celebrates American-style, with a big turkey, or British-style, with a plum pudding, and Santa doesn't actually visit EVERY country in the world.

If you happen to be royalty, like me, it's important to know how cultures other than your own celebrate their special days, or you could make a really big ass out of yourself at some regal function.

Read on to find out how Christmas is enjoyed in other parts of the world:

Australia

Christmas Down Under takes place in the heat of summer, since Australia is located in the southern hemisphere! So some Australians get to have their Christmas dinner on the beach. Which is totally unfair. Palm trees and surfing, at Christmas time? Lucky Australians – they get Father Christmas and summer breeze at the same time!

Belgium

Belgium, known throughout the world for its excellent *pommes frites* (aka French fries), is located between France and the Netherlands. In Belgium, St Nick rides into town on a white horse or donkey. It's Father Christmas who's stuck with the reindeer. Lucky Belgian kids, getting presents from TWO gift-giving dudes.

Brazil

Papai Noel (Father Noel) is the gift-bringer in Brazil. According to legend, he lives in Greenland, but when he arrives in Brazil he strips down to his skivvies, due to the summer heat. On December 25 most everybody goes to church, but the Masses usually take place in the late afternoon, because everyone has to take a nap after their big Ceia de Natal (Christmas dinner), which is held at midday, sometimes on the beach!

Canada

Canadians celebrate Christmas much like the rest of the North Americans do, with the exception being that Canadians also observe Boxing Day, or the Feast of St Stephen, on December 26. Supposedly on this day it was the tradition for poor people to go door to door, carrying empty boxes, which the wealthier filled with food, money and clothes they no longer wanted. Canadian parents are supposed to give their kids small gifts such as oranges, handkerchiefs and socks on Boxing Day. Although I have never seen any evidence of this on *Degrassi*.

Chile

In Chile Santa is known as Viejo Pascuero, or Old Man Christmas. He looks like Santa Claus and he drives a team of reindeer, but since there aren't many chimneys in Chilean homes, due to the warm climate, Viejo Pascuero climbs through the window with his gifts.

He better not try this in New York City, or he might run into a little trouble!

Colombia

Colombians take the holiday season super-seriously! A traditional Colombian Christmas dinner would include *ajïaco* (a soup with potatoes), chicken, *natilla* (a corn-based dessert) and something called *buñuelos*. Traditionally, 'El Niño Jesus' (the Christ Child) is the one who brings kids their gifts, not Santa. Christmas trees in Colombia are almost always fake, for ecological reasons. Go, Colombia, save those fir trees!

Cuba

Cuba is best known, of course, for the movie *Dirty Dancing 2: Havana Nights*. But it's also known for its hard-core Christmas celebrating. As in Spain, gifts are exchanged on the day of Epiphany, King's Day, on January 6. Children's gifts are brought by the Magi, Reyes Magos. Even Communism couldn't quell the Cubans' love of Christmas, and finally Fidel Castro, the reigning dictator, gave up trying. Take that, Señor Castro!

Denmark

Christmas is the most important event on the Danish calendar – in fact, this tiny nation consumes more candles per capita than any other country on earth, mostly at Christmas time (I am sure the New York Fire Department would have a thing or two to say about this). The Danish have a funny tradition involving an almond hidden in a bowl of rice pudding: whoever finds the almond gets a prize. Danish people also supposedly leave a bowl of the rice pudding out for the Julnisse – a mischievous elf who lives in the attic and plays jokes on people in the house. If he gets his pudding, though, he will watch over the household throughout the year. This is sort of like Fat Louie, who gets very cranky when denied his Fancy Feast.

Dubai

Dubai, in the United Arab Emirates, is a multicultural society where it's not unusual to find people sunbathing on one of its many beaches on Christmas Day. In fact, it's a major vacation destination during the holidays. Shopping could almost be described as a national pastime in

Dubai, since some Europeans actually make a special trip to this country to the many festively decorated markets just to do their Christmas shopping (Grandmere is one person I could mention who has been known to do this).

Estonia

In Estonia, most of the holiday action takes place on Christmas Eve. This is when the President of Estonia declares Christmas Peace. Declaring Christmas Peace is a 350-year-old tradition, which began in the seventeenth century by order of Queen Kristina of Sweden. Go, Queen Kristina! The best-known Christmas tradition in Estonia is mumming. Mummers are like mimes in the US, only hopefully not as repulsive or annoying.

France

On Christmas Eve, French children put their shoes (*sabots*) in front of the fireplace, instead of their stockings. But the idea is still the same – that Père Noël (Father Christmas) will fill the shoes with presents (hopefully they'll check before putting their shoes on in the morning, because who wants to get caramel or whatever all over their socks?). Père Noël's partner, Père Fouettard (Father Spanker), 'rewards' bad children with a spanking (France is so kinky!). The family Christmas dinner is followed by a *bûche de Noël*, a traditional French cake baked in the shape of a yule log and decorated to look like one. Another traditional cake served during the holiday season in France is a *roi*, or king cake, served during the feast of the Magi. A small figurine of a king and queen are baked inside the cake, and whichever children get the figurines are king and queen for the day. This would never go over in the US, of course, due to the choking hazard.

Genovia
See 'Christmas in Genovia' (page 57).

Germany
German children are visited by St Nicholas on December 6, when the old guy fills their shoes with candy if they've been good or twigs if they've been bad (ouch). In Germany, it's traditional not to let the children in the house to see the decorated tree until Christmas Eve. This would be very difficult to do in New York City, considering

the size of the apartments here, but whatever. On Christmas Eve, everyone in Germany eats a huge amount of white sausage and macaroni salad, followed on Christmas Day by another huge meal that includes *Christollen* (fruit-and-nut-filled bread) and marzipan.

Then on December 26, everyone goes on Atkins in order to fit into their lederhosen again.

Greece

On Christmas Eve, Greek children go around their neighbourhood singing *kalanda* (Greek carols). They're rewarded with candy by the appreciative Greek households for their efforts (presumably they don't have to take this candy to the local hospital to get it X-rayed for hidden razor blades before eating it the way my mom used to make me do on

Halloween). The Christmas feast afterwards is really important, since Christmas follows forty days of fasting for the Greek Orthodox Church, of which 95 per cent of the country is a member. *Christopsomo* (Christ-bread) is prepared for the meal, and throughout the twelve days of Christmas a fire is kept burning in the fireplace to keep away the Killantzaroi, elfin mischief-makers who turn the milk sour. St Nicholas, not Santa, comes calling on Greek children if they've been good.

Iceland

With a 99.9 per cent literacy rate, you'd expect Icelanders to have some cool customs, and they do. Icelandic Yule is all about family, with everyone pitching in to decorate and celebrate St Thorlakur's Day (named for Iceland's major native saint, Thorlakur Thorhallsson, former Bishop of Skálholt) on December 23. The main custom associated with Thorláksmessa (St Thorlakur's Day) is eating skate (a fish. And, um, yuck). The Yule tree is usually decorated on the evening of this day. The children in Iceland get not one, but thirteen, Santas, known as Jólasveinar. They're supposed to be the tiny descendants of mythological figures known as Grýla the Ogre and Leppalúði. Each one drops by with a gift, starting December 12, but the gifts can't be opened until Christmas Eve. Um, hello, thirteen gifts? I'm so moving to Iceland!!!!

Ireland
Despite what I have observed on St Patrick's Day in the US, Christmas in Ireland is generally more about religion than partying, with an

important significance placed on the lighting of candles, especially in the window (to guide Santa's sleigh. Oh, and also friends who might want to visit), and with manger scenes in most homes (along with Christmas trees, of course). St Stephen's Day is celebrated in Ireland rather than Boxing Day, with pantomimes (plays) the popular choice of entertainment. St Stephen's Day also includes something called the Wren Boys' Procession, in which groups of young people go door to door in costumes, generally demanding pudding (dessert).

I would like to see them try to get away with this in the Bronx.

Israel

While a Jewish state, Israel IS home to Bethlehem, the birthplace of Christ. People come from all over on December 25 to visit the Church of the Nativity, which is said to have been built over what is considered to be the location of Christ's birth, with a fourteen-pointed silver star marking the location of the original manger. Visitors can attend Christmas Eve services there by invitation only, though the service is broadcast on huge television screens in what is known as 'Manger Square'. Just like in Times Square on New Year's! Only with Jesus instead of Dick Clark!

Italy

Christmas in Italy is a combination of Christian tradition blended with the pagan practices of ancient

Rome's winter-solstice celebration ('Saturnalia'), which occurs at the same time as Advent. For instance, Christmas sweets containing nuts and honey are common throughout Italy – panettone, (cake filled with candied fruit) and *torrone* (nougat) – since in ancient Rome, honey was traditionally consumed around the solstice in hopes that the new year would be sweet, and nuts supposedly symbolize fertility (get it?). Though Babbo Natale Santa comes to visit most Italian homes nowadays, traditionally the principal gift-bringer was a dude named La Befana (St Lucia) or Gesu Bambino (Baby Jesus). Lucky Italian kids, with all those people bringing them stuff! No wonder none of them ever wants to leave home.

Korea

Christmas is getting to be a bigger and bigger deal in Korea, with Christmas decorations going up in October and staying up sometimes until March. Just like in the US!

Lithuania

Lithuanians love Christmas trees and, come December, almost every home has a decorated tree. *Prakartelis* (crèche or nativity scenes) are also popular with churches and schools. Lithuanian kids are lucky since they can get gifts twice: once on New Year's Day, from Senis Saltis (Father Frost) when Kaledu Senis (Father Christmas) comes calling, and once on Kucios (Christmas Eve). It's traditional on Christmas Eve in Lithuania for twelve special dishes to be served (representing the twelve months of the year), each containing no fat, milk, butter or meat – the anti-Atkins! On Christmas Day, though, Lithuanians can eat whatever they want.

Mexico

Mexicans love Christmas and are famous for their traditional re-enactments of Joseph and Mary's search for a hotel room. They do this on nine consecutive nights before Christmas, through the ritual of Las Posadas, a procession of children and adults that, as soon as it gets dark, heads through town until they get to the house appointed to be the 'inn' for that night, where the 'innkeeper' invites them in for colaciones (candy) and, for the adults, plenty of tequila. This goes on for eight nights, but on Christmas Eve, the ninth evening, Baby Jesus joins the Holy Family in the *nacimiento*.

I sincerely hope there's a child-safety seat on that donkey.

Monaco

The Principality of Monaco, which borders Genovia, Italy and France, has a Christmas tradition similar to the Genovian 'rite of the olive branch', in that the youngest member of the family is required to soak an olive branch in a glass of grappa, then burn it while saying a bunch of nice things about olives, the country's main form of income (before cruise ships and baccarat came along). They still make the youngest member of the family (namely ME) do this in SOME countries I could mention.

New Zealand

In New Zealand, Santa rides into town on a fire engine, which if you ask me is an abuse of city-owned property. Many people in New Zealand barbecue on Christmas, but some still follow the old English traditions and have turkey and plum pudding – plus a pavlova, a sort of meringue. Some New Zealanders celebrate two Christmases – the second one in July, which is winter for them, complete with a tree. In some homes, a traditional Maori hangi is built outside. This is like a Hawaiian luau, or fire pit, where food is slow-cooked all day. Most of this food is of the non-vegetarian variety, you might not be too surprised to learn.

Philippines

Christmas in the Philippines is all about firecrackers (from Christmas Eve until New Year's), which must be a big headache for Philippino fire departments. Decorating and carolling to raise money for church groups (or to get treats, for kids) is typical. There are town processions, generally church-sponsored, and Christmas dinner is almost always roast pig.

Pigs have the intelligence of a human three-year-old, just to let you know.

Romania

In Romania, children go from house to house on Christmas Eve, singing carols and reciting ancient legends (um, yawn. I mean, fun). Then everyone goes home for *turta*, a special cake made for Nosterea Domnului Isus (also known as Christmas

Eve), which is made up of thin layers of rolled dough to represent the swaddling clothes of the Christ Child (cool). If you've been good, Santa will visit. If not, you get *bupkis*.

Russia

St Nicholas is super-popular in Russia, and the feast of St Nicholas (December 6) is the highlight of the Christmas season for many Russians. Still, it's an old lady named Babushka who brings gifts for most Russian kids. Russians, as we all know, like marching around, so there are lots of Christmas Eve processions, notably the Krestny Khod procession, which is led by the highest-ranking member of the Russian Orthodox Church. After attending Mass, Russians go home to Christmas Eve dinner, which features a porridge called *kutya*, eaten from a common dish to symbolize unity. Rumour has it that if a bit of porridge is thrown against the ceiling and sticks, the harvest will be extra-bounteous. Rock on, Russia.

Singapore

A former British colony, Singapore is a multicultural society that celebrates the festivals of many countries and religions, and Christmas is definitely one of them. Contests are held to see which hotels and businesses have the nicest Christmas displays, and gift exchanges between friends and colleagues are common. But remember, if you live in Singapore and get gum for Christmas, you have to have a special gum-chewing licence to put it in your mouth. (This is not a joke. Although if you think about it, it's actually good because all those black spots you see on the sidewalk in New

York? Gum. Also birds could eat it and their beaks could get stuck together.)

South Africa

In South Africa, school is closed for Christmas – not for one day, but for FIVE WEEKS, because Christmas falls over South African midsummer. Lucky South Africans. Most families celebrate with an outside meal or braai (barbecue), along with swimming or a picnic at the beach. Santa still manages to find his way to South Africa, even though it's summer there in December and he's probably sweating quite a lot.

Switzerland

Because Switzerland is such a mountainous region, the various towns there, isolated from one another for many years, each developed their own unique Christmas customs . . . though most of them centre on St Nicholas. Bell-ringing, parades and carol-singing all the mark the day in various parts of the country. Some other parts of the country, though, might need a little guidance . . . like the town where, on Christmas Eve, young bachelors roam about town behind a sooty rag (or pig's bladder) attached to a pole. In some towns, Christmas traditions such as the pig-bladder one got so wild, they were officially moved to New Year's, so as to help people keep in mind Christmas's roots as a holy day. Excuse me, but couldn't these guys just stay home and play *Doom 3* like normal bachelors?

Trinidad and Tobago

Even though they're located in the Caribbean, Santa still finds his way to Trinidad and Tobago (and who can blame him? The weather is a heck of a lot nicer that time of year than it is at the North Pole). The Christmas season on the islands is very festive, with an emphasis on carolling to steel drums and tambourines (parang – the music of the Caribbean). Christmas dinner may include *pastelles* (beef-filled pastries), and dessert is a special cake soaked in Caribbean rum for several weeks. Sometimes more. Sometimes an extra dash of rum is added to the already rum-soaked cake. I'm just reporting what I've heard.

United Kingdom

They've been celebrating Christmas in the home of the author of *A Christmas Carol* since King Arthur's time, maybe even longer, so they pretty much have it down by now. It's not ENTIRELY about that Christmas pudding Bob Cratchit's family anticipates so eagerly in *A Christmas Carol*, although puddings are still pretty popular . . . as are Christmas trees, a tradition brought to Britain by Queen Victoria's husband, Prince Albert, from his native Germany. Santa Claus, known in England as Father Christmas, visits overnight on Christmas Eve. Just like in Genovia, the ruling monarch addresses the common people over the airwaves to assure them all is right with the kingdom. And on Boxing Day, the day after Christmas, everyone takes time out to see a pantomime, which can involve large puppets, like the pantomime Princess Margaret frequently seen on *Monty Python*, a favourite show of Mr Gianini's for reasons neither my mother nor I can understand.

United States of America

See 'Christmas in New York' (page 50) and 'Christmas in Indiana' (page 62).

Venezuela

On December 16 the Christmas season officially begins in lovely Venezuela when families bring out their *presebres* (nativity scenes) and display them. These can sometimes feature things not included at the original nativity, such as electric trains, boats and cartoon figures like Bart Simpson or action figures like Lara Croft of *Tomb Raider*. But Venezuelans are big on imagination and won't be hemmed in by convention. Venezuelan children are left gifts Christmas morning by the Christ Child or Santa. But the good stuff usually comes on January 6, the Epiphany, or Day of the Reyes

Magos (Three Wise Men), who drop in with candy to signify the end of the Christmas season.

Mmmm, candy.

CHRISTMAS IN HOLLYWOOD
Lilly and Mia's Guide to the Top Ten Holiday Movies
By Lilly Moscovitz and Mia Thermopolis

OK, OK, so the holidays are SUPPOSED to be about spending time with family and not about watching movies.

Well, we discovered a long time ago that a great way to spend time with your family is to spend it WATCHING MOVIES. Yes! That way, there is no fighting – except maybe over which movie to watch.

That's why we've composed this helpful list, so in the future you won't have to fight – you can just pull out the list and use it to persuade others of the superiority of your film choice over theirs.

Here goes:

10. 'Groundhog Day'
Although technically this a movie that takes place on February 2, or Groundhog Day, it still has a very holidayish feel to it, since it's very funny and uplifting and is all about living life to its fullest and helping others, which is really what the holidays are all about. Plus, Bill Murray is just hilarious.

9. 'The Ref'
Denis Leary plays a thief who gets trapped in a house on Christmas Eve with what is perhaps the most dysfunctional family ever documented on film. As you might expect, this chain-smoking, foul-mouthed criminal knows more about the

Christmas spirit than the horrible, supposedly loving family he is trapped with, and ends up teaching them a thing or two about love and family loyalty. Plus, it contains the immortal quote: 'Kid, gag your grandma.'

8. 'Home for the Holidays'

Jody Foster directed this funny and touching movie about a down-and-out single mom (Holly Hunter) who goes home to visit her parents for Thanksgiving and ends up alienating her sister while bonding closer with her gay brother, fabulously played by Robert Downey Jr. (who seems to ad-lib most, if not all, of his lines). Even better? A pre-*The Practice* Dylan McDermott plays Holly Hunter's love interest.

7. 'Scrooged'

Another Bill Murray movie, only this one really DOES take place over Christmas. A modern retelling of Charles Dickens's *A Christmas Carol*, in this version Scrooge is a TV executive who sold his soul (practically) to be rich and famous. Karen Allen stars as the perky social worker he left behind. Carol Kane is hilarious as an abusive Ghost of Christmas Present.

6. 'Scrooge' (1970 musical)

This ANCIENT film starring Albert Finney features many songs that you will recognize, such as 'Thank You Very Much' and 'I Like Life'. Well, OK, maybe you won't recognize them, but by the end you'll be humming them. This is by far the best version of *A Christmas Carol* that we know of, and one of the few with DANCING in it, so that it makes it far superior to its non-dancing cousins. Plus it has the best line of any Christmas movie ever: 'I want the dolly in the corner!' Say it a few times with an English accent. Go ahead. We DARE you.

5. 'It's a Wonderful Life' (aka 'Frank Capra's It's a Wonderful Life')

This is a fabulous movie about a man who wishes he had never existed and gets his wish (don't worry, it has a happy ending). It's a movie that begs many questions, such as, Is it possible to watch this movie without crying at the end? And, How does one spell ZuZu? And, Why can't Donna Reed be MY mother? The part when Jimmy Stewart grabs her and says he doesn't want plastics is actually way hot, for a Christmas movie.

4. 'The Santa Clause'

We hate to admit it, but this movie is a bit of a guilty pleasure, enjoyable even if you AREN'T seven years old. Tim Allen plays a man who inherits the role of Santa – the REAL Santa – and is none too pleased about porking out and having to move to the North Pole . . . though his son couldn't be more delighted. This movie answers a lot of those questions that have bothered us, such as, How does Santa get to every house in one night? And, Does he really eat all those cookies? Satisfying as Oreos and a glass of milk.

3. 'Die Hard'

A lot of people forget this is a Christmas movie, but that's the whole reason Bruce Willis is visiting his wife in the first place. See, she moved to LA for a fancy new job, while her husband stayed in New York to be a cop. So he's coming home for the holidays to patch things up, and – as usually happens – Eurotrash terrorists choose Christmas Eve to take everyone in his wife's office hostage. Bruce has to save the day . . . and, not to give anything away, but he survives to make *Die Hard 2*.

2. 'National Lampoon's Christmas Vacation'

This movie is the silly antidote to all the sappy Suzanne Somers made-for-TV holiday movies you've been watching (don't even try to deny it). Chevy Chase doesn't get the Christmas bonus he'd counted on receiving in order to build his family a pool, and he goes a little insane. But you can understand why after you meet his in-laws. Not to mention the squirrel in the Christmas tree.

And the number one Christmas movie of all time . . .

1. 'A Christmas Story'

This movie is written by a guy from Indiana, and also set there, but the story of his main character Ralphie's obsession with owning a Daisy air rifle is familiar to us all, Hoosier or not (only for Mia it was Prom-Dress Barbie; for Lilly, an electromagnetic microscope). Ralphie's endeavours to be good so he can earn his rifle, his fantasies about what he'll do when he gets his rifle, his painful trip to see Santa to ask for the rifle and his adventures along the way all speak to the heart of what Christmas is all about in the eyes of a child. Speaking of eyes, the best line in the whole movie? 'Yellow eyes! He had yellow eyes!' Hasn't every kid in the world been menaced by a yellow-eyed bully? What's UP with that???

VI. Xmas Xtras

A Note from Her Royal Highness, Princess Mia Thermopolis

Just like you can never have enough wrapping paper, you can never have enough of Christmas.

Well, OK, maybe you can. Like after you've eaten the entire contents of your Christmas stocking AND the candy canes off the tree AND watched *The Little Drummer Boy* seventeen times in a row. Not that I've ever done this.

Not more than once a year, anyway.

ADVENT
Somebody Bring Me a Sidecar
By Grandmere, Dowager Princess of Genovia
[with commentary by the Princess herself]

Advent takes place during the period beginning the
Sunday closest to the feast of St Andrew and ending Christmas Day. It is thought that the four weeks

of Advent symbolize the four thousand years of darkness in which the world was enveloped before the birth of Jesus Christ, although there is no liturgical confirmation of this of which I am aware.

Advent is a time of preparing for the anniversary of the Lord's coming on December 25. Many might confuse this with Yule, which has its roots in pagan worship. Nothing could be further from the truth. Although it is true that by the time Advent arrives there are very few shopping days for Christmas left, and when Yule arrives there are even FEWER, and one might as well just give up all hope of using anything but Overnight Express if you want it to get there in time for Christmas.

So true.

Princess Party Tip

You don't have to own a calendar made by Fabergé in the shape of the Genovian palace (with windows that really open to reveal a jewel inside to represent each of the days of Advent) to celebrate the four weeks of Advent. You can make your own Advent calendar! To do so, you will need:

+ big piece of felt
+ another piece of felt
+ glue
+ scissors
+ fabric marker

Cut out twenty-eight small pieces of felt (each approximately the size and shape of a postage stamp). Then cut out one big piece of felt, big enough to fit all twenty-eight of the small pieces. Glue the sides and bottom of the small pieces of felt in four rows of seven across the big piece of felt, leaving the top of each open.

After numbering the pockets you've created

with the fabric marker, fill the twenty-eight pockets with something of your choice: clues to a scavenger hunt around the house, leading to a small prize; nuts or hard candies; money; slips of paper with lyrics from Christmas carols or a Biblical quote written on them; video-game tokens; pieces of a puzzle.

Each day, pull one object from the pocket corresponding to that day, until you reach December 25. Fun for the whole family!

Enjoy!

THE CHRISTMAS TREE
Dead Celebrities Have Their Due
By Helen Thermopolis, Celebrated Painter and
Mother of Princess Mia Thermopolis
[with commentary by the Princess herself]

Is there anything that lifts the spirits more than the sight of a Christmas tree? Even people in ancient times hung evergreens around their peat-moss huts, in order to remind themselves that spring, a time when everything turns green again, was around the corner.

Is it any wonder the tradition stuck?

Druids were among the first to place fir trees in their homes in the dead of winter as a symbol of everlasting life. Martin Luther, a founder of the Protestant faith, is said to be the first to have had the idea of decorating his fir tree, an idea that came to him as he walked through the woods one night and noticed how shiny the ice crystals hanging from the branches were in the moonlight. So he placed candles on the ends of each branch of his own tree indoors to replicate the glistening icicles he'd seen.

Today, this effect is much more economically — and safely — accomplished with twinkly lights and/or tinsel. The use of open flames anywhere near evergreens is frowned upon by the NYFD.

While the Christmas tree in the Genovian palace might sparkle with lovely bejewelled and priceless ornaments, I have always found that the most beautiful – and meaningful – decorations are those made by the hands of friends or family members, because those decorations are made with the rarest jewel of all: love.

Princess Party Tip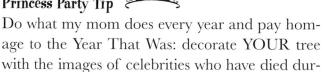

Do what my mom does every year and pay homage to the Year That Was: decorate YOUR tree with the images of celebrities who have died during the course of the previous year.

To make your own Dead Celebrity tree you will need:

+ 1 tree
+ magazines
+ scissors
+ glue
+ cardboard
+ thread

Look through magazines for images of Dead Celebrities. When you find one you like, cut it out. Glue it to some cardboard. Trim the cardboard. Poke a hole through the top. Tie it to a branch with thread. Voila! Your own Dead Celebrity tree.

Enjoy!

THE CAROLS
Good King Wenceslas, Victim of Fratricide
By Boris Pelkowski, Musical Genius and Mouthbreather
[with commentary by Princess Mia Thermopolis]

Throughout history, music has always played an important part of any celebration. We sing and play instruments to express our greatest joys (and sometimes sorrows). Our earliest ancestors realized this, and that's why many of our most beloved Christmas carols actually got their start as age-old chants or hymns, folk songs created by simple peasants, since singing in the church was forbidden for many years.

It was St Francis of Assisi who recognized the importance of song in the celebration of life, and who brought these folk songs into the formal worship of the church during a Christmas Midnight Mass in a cave in Greccio, in the province of Umbria, in 1223. These songs were then spread across the land by wandering minstrels who travelled from hamlet to castle, performing them in exchange for alms (money).

In a time when few people knew how to read (and even fewer books were actually printed) song was an important teaching tool. The popular carol Good King Wenceslas actually memorializes a real historical figure, a Bohemian king who was murdered in 929 CE by his own brother (and whose mother murdered his grandmother. You might say it ran in the family). Through song, the memory of Wenceslas lives on, teaching his lesson of being kind to one's neighbours.

Today, many people still go 'carolling' in order to spread holiday cheer and joy. I hope, however, that they don't get their hopes up about getting any 'alms', because the last time I went carolling, all I got were a few pennies and a piece of raisin bread. Although that might have been because I was playing Bartók. But still.

I know. You've heard 'Jingle Bell Rock' so many times you're ready to rip off your own ears. But here are some Christmas selections you won't get tired of (at least, not right away):

114

- 'Mr Hankey's Christmas Classics' (South Park)
- 'Punk Rock Christmas' (various artists/punk)
- 'You Sleigh Me' (various artists/alternative)
- 'Christmas with the Rat Pack' (Frank Sinatra, Sammy Davis Jr., Dean Martin)
- 'My Kind of Christmas' (Christina Aguilera)

Don't be dissing Xtina, she's got like a seven-octave range, for God's sake.

And don't forget the Muppets and 'A Charlie Brown Christmas', for those times you're feeling insanely 70s.

Princess Party Tip

If carollers show up at your house or apartment, don't be a grinch! It's polite to offer them a small donation if they are carolling for charity, or at least a warm drink. Bringing them a figgy pudding isn't necessary, but remember the 'we won't go until we get some' line. Better safe than sorry.

THE TRUTH ABOUT ST NICK

aka Santa Claus, Kris Kringle, Christkind, Père Noël, St Nicholas, Papa Noël, Father Christmas, Old Man Christmas, Befana, Santa Kurohsu

By Artur Christoff Phillipe Gerard Grimaldi Renaldo, Prince of Genovia and father of Princess Mia Thermopolis [with commentary by the Princess herself]

Many people assume (erroneously) that St Nicholas (Sinterklaus or Santa Claus) was a fat jolly man who, part elf, achieved immortality and currently lives at the North Pole with his wife and some reindeer.

Nothing could be further from the truth. A powerful bishop who at one time was thrown into prison, Nicholas of Myra believed strongly in helping young people (particularly young brides in need of a dowry). He was like a one-man scholarship fund, often dropping bags of gold anonymously down the chimney when he knew a young lady's father did not approve of her match.

Because of this generosity, Nicholas was declared a saint . . . but, like many popular leaders, he was not allowed to rest, even after his death. His remains were said to have miraculous healing properties and were eventually stolen from his tomb in his native land, which is why today they are stored in the beautiful Basilica of St Nicholas at Bari in Italy.

EW!!! THEY TOUCHED HIS BONES!!!!

During the Reformation in the sixteenth century, attempts to make people forget about St Nicholas were unsuccessful – as attempts to make anyone forget the kindnesses of a past ruler often are. The people could never forget such a kind and thoughtful regent. The Church tried to replace Nicholas with the 'Christkind' (Christchild, which later became Kris Kringle), who placed nuts and candies in the shoes of children who had been good throughout the year. Good behaviour on the part of children has been rewarded by parents, in the guise of St Nicholas, ever since – much in the way that productive members of society receive a tax refund from the government at the end of the year, except in Genovia, where, of course, there are no taxes, due to the benefaction of a certain current regent.

Modern-day Santa probably comes from an illustration from an 1870 edition of *A Visit from Saint Nicholas*, in which St Nicholas is depicted wearing a red coat. This image has, of course, been reinforced by hundreds of thousands of illustrations ever since, but probably has absolutely no relation to how the real Nicholas looked or dressed – much like the image of me on the currency of Genovia bears no real likeness to how I appear today, since shaving my moustache.

Um, and losing all your hair.

And let us not forget what is probably the most enduring image of Santa to American children: the scary shopping-mall Santa, whose lap we are required to sit on. Why do these Santas always smell funny? And why did he never bring me the Prom-Dress Barbie I wanted?

THE CHRISTMAS STAR
White Dwarf or Jupiter in Retrograde?
By Kenny Showalter, Conspiracy Theorist and Biology Lab Partner of Princess Mia Thermopolis

While many assume the Star of Bethlehem was only a myth, some of us disagree. Some of us, in fact, have spent many, many hours analysing data from the numerous astronomical events around the time of Jesus's birth that could have provided the star the Three Wise Men *(aka the Magi, or astrologers, as some New Testament translations explicitly call them — later translations bumped them up to 'king' status)* followed to Bethlehem.

Our research has led to some startling theories that could, should they become more widely known, shake the foundations of Santaland as we know it.

CONJUNCTION. There were three extremely rare conjunctions *(a conjunction is when two or more objects appear very close together in the sky)* of planets around the time of Jesus's birth: one in May, when the Wise Men would have started out on their journey; the second in late September, when they were visiting King Herod; and the third in early

December, over Bethlehem, when they would have been leaving Herod's palace. Though Jupiter and Saturn never got close enough together to be confused as a single object, the word for star may have had a different definition than it does today. *WAS IT A CONJUNCTION THE WISE MEN SAW????*

NOVA. While the exact time of Jesus's birth is not known, Chinese astronomers recorded a new star (nova) in the constellation Capricorn around the time he is thought to have been born. This star is said to have been visible for over two months. Novas are caused by dying stars *(so the term 'new star' is erroneous, as they are actually very old stars)* which sometimes become white dwarves, due to thermonuclear reactions on the surface as the stars die, which flare very brightly, then fade from view in a few months. Possibly it was a nova the Wise Men were following.

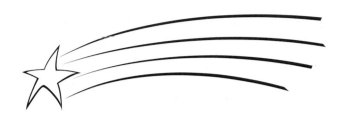

METEOR (SHOOTING STAR), COMET. A meteor lasts only a few seconds or minutes at best. The Wise Men followed the star for weeks looking for Jesus, so it couldn't have been a shooting star. We can rule out comets for the same reason. They are not stationary for long enough for the Wise Men to have followed one for as long as they did, therefore ruling out this theory. *(HA! I told you shooting-star theorists your idea was lame!)*

JUPITER IN RETROGRADE. Many astronomers feel the 'star' was simply Jupiter undergoing retrograde motion. *(Going backwards: stars and planets do this sometimes, the same way I sometimes put my shirts* *on backwards and don't realize it until I get to school.)* While in retrograde, the planet appears to be stationary for about a week. Jupiter in retrograde, while ALSO in a conjunction with other planets (see first theory), would have been the brightest point in the sky, besides the moon, at that time, and COULD be the star the Wise Men were following.

The above are just SOME of the many, many theories out there that could explain the Star of Bethlehem. Could there be other, as yet unexplored, explanations? Oh yes, my friend. And while some people suggest it's better not to examine the science behind historical miracles, as the findings can be disappointing, I, however, disagree, at least so far as the Christmas star is concerned. To me, as to the ancients who recorded its viewing, the star symbolizes hope – and isn't that what Christmas is all about?

That is so sweet, Kenny! But, I'm sorry, you'd better not be hoping that I'm going to the Non-Denominational Winter Dance with you.

VII. Celebrating Kwanzaa

A Note from Her Royal Highness Princess Mia Thermopolis

There aren't many holidays that were invented by an actual person, as opposed to a group of people, like the Maccabees or the Romans. That isn't true about Kwanzaa, though, because it was invented by Dr Maulana Karenga. When I take over the throne of Genovia, one of the first things I'm going to do is invent my own holiday. It's going to be called Mia Day, and on Mia Day everybody has to go to their local animal shelter and adopt a pet.

Unless they have a cat like Fat Louie at home, who might rip any other pet in his vicinity to shreds. Then they can just go to the animal shelter and take a stray dog for a walk and return him later, or something. Because I don't want to cause any pet-icides.

THREE CHEERS FOR KWANZAA

By Shameeka Taylor, Albert Einstein
High School Cheerleader
[with commentary by Princess Mia Thermopolis]

Kwanzaa is another mid-winter celebration like Christmas or Hanukkah, only Kwanzaa doesn't have a religious basis. Instead, it's a unique

African-American celebration that focuses on the traditional African values of family, community responsibility, commerce and self-improvement. It's a time for people, especially African Americans, to reaffirm their culture and ancestral heritage.

Kwanzaa is based on the Nguzo Saba (seven guiding principles), one for each day of the observance, and is celebrated from December 26 to January 1. Because the names of the days of Kwanzaa are in the African language of Kiswahili, I created a cheer about them, since they can sometimes be difficult to remember. Just shout the word and its meaning in a very loud voice, preferably while jumping up and down with pom-poms:

Umoja (OO-MO-JAH) – Unity!
Kujichagulia (KOO-GEE-CHA-GOO-LEE-YAH) – Self-determination!

Ujima (OO-GEE-MAH) – Responsibility!
Ujamaa (OO-JAH-MAH) – Cooperation!
Nia (NEE-YAH) – Purpose!
Kuumba (KOO-OOM-BAH) – Creativity!
Imani (EE-MAH-NEE) – Faith!

Don't worry if the neighbours ask you to keep it down. Just tell them you're celebrating Kwanzaa, which they will probably know anyway because your home will be decorated in the colors of Kwanzaa (black, red and green).

What about the gifts? Aren't there PRESENTS?

It is traditional to give creative or artistic gifts – preferably homemade – on the last day of Kwanzaa, January 1.

In other words, a Segway Human Transporter would not be an appropriate Kwanzaa gift.

Ready? OK: KWANZAA YENU IWE NA HERI! (HAPPY KWANZAA!)

Princess Party Tip

Hold your own Kwanzaa Karumu (the Kwanzaa feast traditionally held on December 31)! A typical Kwanzaa menu should include traditional African dishes such as peanut soup, chicken stew, sweet-potato fritters, couscous and fried plantains. A fun recipe you can try at home is benne cakes. Benne (which means sesame seed) cakes are from west Africa, where sesame seeds are eaten for good luck.

To make Benne Cakes, grease a cookie sheet with oil and preheat your oven to 170°C, 325°F, gas mark 3. Then gather up:

+ 1 cup finely packed brown sugar
  (1 cup = 200 ml / 8 fl. oz)

+ ¼ cup butter or margarine, softened

- 1 egg
- ½ tsp vanilla extract
- ½ tsp freshly squeezed lemon juice
- ½ cup plain flour
- ½ tsp baking powder
- ¼ tsp salt
- 1 cup toasted sesame seeds (take raw sesame seeds and dry-fry them until they turn golden and give off a nutty smell)

Mix together the brown sugar and butter or margarine, and beat until they are creamy. Stir in the egg, vanilla extract and lemon juice. Add the flour, baking powder, salt and sesame seeds, and mix well. Drop by rounded teaspoons on to the cookie sheet 2 inches apart. Bake for 15 minutes or until the edges are browned.

Enjoy!

VIII. HAPPY NEW YEAR

A Note from Her Royal Highness Princess Mia Thermopolis

As everyone knows, New Year's is the day marking the end of the previous year's calendar and the beginning of a new one. This is one of the most ancient of all the holidays, beginning in Babylon about four THOUSAND years ago.

Of course, back then they didn't have Times Square to drop the ball in, or even Dick Clark, so the Babylonians celebrated by slaughtering a bunch of innocent animals and eating them. Probably a few virgins too.

The slaughtering, I mean. Not the eating.

Most cultures held their new-year festivities on the spring solstice – a sign that winter was over and a new agricultural season was beginning. A lot of the new-year traditions we practise today are the same ones practised by the ancient civilizations before us. Who knew making a New Year's resolution – such as not biting your fingernails any more – is actually very Babylonian? I had no idea I was so cosmopolitan!

BABY NEW YEAR
Call Child Protective Services!
By Rocky Thermopolis-Gianini
Baby Brother to Princess Mia Thermopolis
[with translation and commentary by the Princess herself]

Goo goo gee mwah fa la la la, twee goo.

Since Rocky is still a baby and can't speak English properly, I will translate. Here he is saying: The tradition of using a baby to symbolize the new year is actually Greek. It was traditional in 600 BCE to parade around on New Year's with a baby in a basket. The baby was supposed to be Dionysus, the god of wine, reborn for the new year.

I would just like to say that this is a very irresponsible way to treat a baby. I hope those baskets had safety belts.

Gew! Gwah ma dee lo FO!

Here Rocky is saying that the Greeks weren't the only ones who used a baby to represent rebirth. The Egyptians did too.

This is very irresponsible of them as well.

Dum do dee fwah goo.

Rocky says the tradition of using a baby to represent the birth of a new year carried on through countless gener-

ations until it reached today's greetings-card industry who have used it almost to death. Thank you, Rocky, for your keen insight into this horrible abuse of babies throughout history.

Goo!

Rocky says, You're welcome!

NEW YEAR'S KISS
When Harry Frenched Sally
By Tina Hakim Baba, Romance Expert

Everyone who's seen the movie *When Harry Met Sally* knows how vitally important it is that you kiss someone special at the stroke of midnight on New Year's Eve.

But does everyone know WHY it's so impor tant?

Traditionally, it's always been thought that what a person does on the first day of the year will affect his or her luck throughout the REST of that year. To this day, many people throughout the world believe that if you eat a certain food – doughnuts in Denmark; ham or black-eyed peas in the southern US; cabbage or rice elsewhere – you will have luck in the new year.

In olden times, some cultures believed that if their first visitor of the year was a tall dark-haired man, they would have good luck. It is no mystery why so many heroes in romance novels are tall, dark and handsome! For centuries, tall, dark and handsome men have been considered sought-after houseguests on New Year's Day.

Kissing someone you love romantically on the stroke of midnight on New Year's Eve is also con-sidered lucky, and bodes well for the health of your relationship. Kissing a guy on New Year's Eve, however, doesn't necessarily mean you will still be with him on the FOLLOWING New Year's.

But it's definitely a start!

AULD LANG SYNE
Oldie But Goodie

By Boris Pelkowksi, Musical Genius and Mouthbreather
[with commentary by Princess Mia Thermopolis]

We've all heard party guests singing the song 'Auld Lang Syne' at New Year's. But does anyone really know what it means, or why people sing it?

At least partially written by the poet Robert Burns in the eighteenth century, 'Auld Lang Syne' was first published after Burns's death in 1796. But the song actually has its roots much earlier – Robert Burns just came up with the modern rendition. 'Auld Lang Syne' is Scottish for 'old long ago', or simply, 'the good old days'. When people sing it, they are saying, 'Don't forget the good times we had in Gifted and Talented class,' or something similar.

The actual words are:

Should auld acquaintance be forgot
and never brought to mind?
Should auld acquaintance be forgot
and days of auld lang syne?
For auld lang syne, my dear,
for auld lang syne,
we'll take a cup of kindness yet,
for auld lang syne.

This is not unlike the Girl Scout song 'Make new friends, but keep the old. One is silver, and the other gold'. Which is how I feel about Lilly and Tina. Not that any of us were ever Girl Scouts, due to no one's mom ever wanting to be the troop leader.

RESOLUTIONS
'Doom 3' Is an Excellent Game

By Michael Moscovitz,
Royal Consort to the Princess of Genovia
[with commentary by the Princess herself]

People have been making New Year's resolutions for approximately four thousand years. The first to do so were the Babylonians, who used the new year as a reminder to return their neighbours' farm equipment.

Today's resolutions are generally more personal in nature, from resolving to lose weight or get in shape, quit smoking, give up junk food or spend less time playing *Doom 3* and more quality time with your girlfriend.

Although if your girlfriend would just take the time to learn how to play *Doom 3*, then the two of you could play it TOGETHER, and spend more quality time with each other while at the same time fighting off the massive demonic invasion that has overwhelmed the Union Aerospace Corporation (UAC) Mars Research Facility, leaving chaos and horror in its wake, of which you are one of the few survivors . . .

I am not learning how to play that game, OK??? It's stupid and boring! And there are no girls in it!

Actually, there are girls in it, if you would just—

I'll tell you what: I'll play 'Doom 3' with you if you'll play 'Dance Dance Revolution Party' with me.

As I was saying, New Year's is the perfect time to amend behaviours or traits that might be keeping you from becoming the fully self-actualized individual you have always yearned to be. Don't let the fact that researchers say most people abandon their New Year's resolutions less than three weeks after January 1 stop you. Record your resolutions here as a reminder to yourself.

And let go of that joystick!

My New Year's Resolutions

I resolve in the new year to:

_____

_____

_____

_____

_____

_____

_____

HOW TO SAY HAPPY NEW YEAR
AROUND THE GLOBE
Learn This or Else

By Grandmere, Dowager Princess of Genovia

A princess knows that good manners are a
MUST while entertaining. Nothing breaks the

ice at a peace summit or cocktail party faster than greeting someone in his or her native language. With the following guide, you will be able to wish anyone, from a backpacking tourist to a foreign ambassador, Happy New Year with culture and panache. Start memorizing, please:

Afghani	Saale Nao Mubbarak
Afrikaans	Gelukkige nuwe jaar
Albanian	Gëzuar Vitin e Ri
Arabic	Antum salimun
Bengali	Shuvo Nabo Barsho
Bulgarian	Chestita nova godina
Chinese	Chu Shen Tan
Corsican	Pace e Salute
Croatian	Sretna Nova godina
Cymraeg (Welsh)	Blwyddyn Newydd Dda
Czech	Scastny Novy Rok
Danish	Godt Nytår
Dutch	Gelukkig Nieuwjaar
Estonian	Head uut aastat
Finnish	Onnellista Uutta Vuotta

French	Bonne Année
Gaelic	Bliadhna mhath ur
German	Prosit Neujahr
Greek	Kenourios Chronos
Hawaiian	Hauoli Makahiki Hou
Hebrew	L'Shannah Tovah
Hindi	Nahi varsh ka shub kamna
Hungarian	Boldog új évet
Icelandic	Farsælt komandi ár
Indonesian	Selamat Tahun Baru
Inuit	Kiortame pivdluaritlo
Iraqi	Sanah Jadidah
Irish	Bliain nua fe mhaise dhuit
Italian	Felice anno nuovo
Japanese	Akimashite Omedetto Gozaimasu
Kannada	Hosa Varushadha Shubhashayagalu
Khmer	Sua Sdei tfnam tmei
Kisii	Somwaka Omoyia Omuya
Laotian	Sabai dee pee mai
Malay	Selamat Tahun Baru
Maltese	Is-Senal-Tajba
Nepalese	Nawa Barsha ko Shuvakamana
Norwegian	Godt Nyttår
Papuan	Nupela yia i go long yu

Pilipino	Manigong Bagong Taon
Polish	Szczęśliwego Nowego Roku
Portuguese	Feliz Ano Novo
Punjabi	Nave sal di mubarak
Romanian	An nou fericit
Russian	S Novim Godom
Serbo-Croatian	Sretna nova godina
Sindhi	Nayou Saal Mubbarak Hoje
Singhalese	Subha Aluth Awrudhak Vewa
Slovak	A stastlivy Novy Rok
Somali	Iyo Sanad Cusub Oo Fiican
Spanish	Feliz Año Nuevo
Swahili	Heri Za Mwaka Mpya
Swedish	Gott nytt år
Sudanese	Warsa Enggal
Tamil	Eniya Puthandu Nalvazhthukkal
Telegu	Noothana samvatsara shubhakankshalu
Thai	Sawadee Pee Mai
Turkish	Yiliniz Kutlu Olsun
Ukrainian	Shchastlyvoho Novoho Roku
Urdu	Naya Saal Mubbarak Ho
Uzbek	Yangi Yil Bilan
Vietnamese	Chuc Mung Tan Nien

IX. Chinese New Year

A Note from Her Royal Highness Princess MiaThermopolis

I have traditionally spent New Year's Eve at my friend Lilly's apartment, viewing either a James Bond, Arnold Schwarzenegger or *Die Hard* movie marathon, and making our own ice-cream creations, such as Times Square Eclair (Twinkies stuffed with vanilla ice cream and sprinkled with red, white and blue nonpareils) or Dick Clark Clark Bars (ice cream with Clark Bars crumbled over it, then refrozen in various shapes, some of them quite phallic).

Most often, I wake on the morning of New Year's Day with a feeling that I've forgotten something . . . and then I remember.

My teeth. I never brushed them the night before. Ew. Clark Bar plaque.

But other cultures, such as the Chinese, celebrate New Year's in a very different fashion . . . and not even, it turns out, on the same night every year. And there's not a Clark Bar to be seen . . .

WHAT'S YOUR SIGN?

An Interview between Princess Mia Thermopolis and
Ling Su Wong, Blossoming Artist and Chinese American

Mia: Ling Su, I am very interested in Chinese New Year. What can you tell me about it?

Ling Su: Well, Mia, Chinese New Year is different than Western New Year – it falls on a different date every year, since the Chinese calendar is based on astronomical observations of the movement of the sun, the stars and the lunar cycle, making it the longest chronological record in history, and actually more accurate than the Western calendar, which is kind of random on account of different world leaders or popes sticking days in here and there throughout history.

Chinese New Year starts on the first

day of the first New Moon of the new year and ends on the full moon fifteen days later.

Mia: Is this when you set off the firecrackers?

Ling Su: Chinese New Year may seem to Westerners to be about lighting firecrackers, since a lot of that goes on in Chinatown during our New Year's celebration. However, Chinese New Year is really about celebrating the coming of spring, as well as uniting living relatives with those relatives who have passed away – in other words, honouring our ancestors. A feast is prepared in remembrance of those ancestors who have left us, often with place settings laid for them.

Mia: So why do you set off the firecrackers?

Ling Su: Firecrackers are lit for a number of reasons. Nobody really knows which is the real one. One reason may be that the noise supposedly wakes up the dragon who brings the spring rain for the crops. Another belief is that the sound of the fireworks is supposed to scare away evil spirits and misfortunes. In this way, evil will be prevented from coming into the new year.

Mia: What about all those little red envelopes I see lying around Chinatown after New Year's?

Ling Su: They are part of an old custom called Hong Bao (Red Packet), in which married couples and the elderly give money in red envelopes (the colour red is known to ward away evil) to children for luck in the new year.

Mia: This sounds like a very excellent custom that should be incorporated here in the US.

Ling Su: Totally. I raked it in last year.

Anyway, the Chinese don't just have their own special New Year's. They also have their own zodiac, different from the one known to the Western world. Instead of being based on the constellations or the twelve months of the year, the Chinese zodiac is based on a twelve-YEAR cycle. This is on account of Buddha. The way the story goes, when Buddha called all the animals of China to his bedside, only twelve came. Because he wanted to honour the animals for their devotion, he created a year for each animal. The twelve animals that showed up at the Buddha's side were the rat, ox, tiger, hare (rabbit), dragon, snake, horse, sheep (goat), monkey, rooster, dog and pig.

Each of these animals has its own

special characteristics – but they may not be the characteristics you'd expect from that animal. Many Chinese people believe that individuals born into a certain year will grow up to have qualities and personality traits of that year's animal.

Mia: No way! That is SO cool. So I could be a Taurus AND something else? Show me!

Ling Su: Here's a chart. Find the year of your birth, then the animal that corresponds to that year. Remember that Chinese New Year doesn't fall on January 1 – so if you were born in January or February, you might actually fall under the **PREVIOUS** year's sign, depending on when Chinese New Year fell that year. To find out, you can go to http://chinese.astrology.com and click on 'Find your Chinese sign'.

1948, 1960, 1972,1984, 1996, 2008
YEAR OF THE RAT
The Rat is charming, bright, creative and thrifty.
Best love match: Dragon or Monkey
Famous Rats: Gwyneth Paltrow, Eminem, Ben Affleck, Prince Harry

1949, 1961, 1973, 1985, 1997, 2009
YEAR OF THE OX
The Ox is steadfast, dependable and methodical.
Best love match: Snake or Rooster
Famous Oxen: Neve Campbell, Zac Hanson, Meg Ryan, Walt Disney

1950, 1962, 1974, 1986, 1998, 2010
YEAR OF THE TIGER
The Tiger is dynamic, sincere and a leader.
Best love match: Horse or Dog
Famous Tigers: Jodie Foster, Tom Cruise, Ryan Phillippe, Mary-Kate and Ashley Olsen

1951, 1963, 1975, 1987, 1999, 2011
YEAR OF THE HARE/RABBIT
The Rabbit is humble, artistic, long-lived and clear-sighted.

Best love match: Sheep/Goat or Pig

Famous Rabbits: Drew Barrymore, Brad Pitt, Tobey Maguire, Albert Einstein

1952, 1964, 1976, 1988, 2000, 2012
YEAR OF THE DRAGON
The Dragon is flamboyant, lucky and imaginative.

Best love match: Rat or Monkey

Famous Dragons: Sandra Bullock, J.C. Chasez, Freddie Prinze Jr., Robin Williams

1953, 1965, 1977, 1989, 2001, 2013
YEAR OF THE SNAKE
The Snake is discreet, refined and intelligent.

Best love match: Ox or Rooster

Famous Snakes: Sarah Michelle Gellar, Shakira, Sarah Jessica Parker, Abraham Lincoln

1954, 1966, 1978, 1990, 2002, 2014
YEAR OF THE HORSE
The Horse is social, down to earth and appealing to others.
Best love match: Tiger or Dog
Famous Horses: Cindy Crawford, Meg Cabot, Harrison Ford, Oprah Winfrey

1955, 1967, 1979, 1991, 2003, 2015
YEAR OF THE SHEEP/GOAT
The Sheep/Goat is artistic, fastidious, caring and forgiving.
Best love match: Hare/Rabbit, Pig or Sheep/Goat
Famous Sheep/Goats: Matt LeBlanc, Claire Danes, Julia Roberts, Michelangelo

1956, 1968, 1980, 1992, 2004, 2016
YEAR OF THE MONKEY
The monkey is witty, popular, good-humoured and versatile.
Best love match: Rat or Dragon
Famous Monkeys: Christina Aguilera, Halle Berry, Will Smith, Charles Dickens

1957, 1969, 1981, 1993, 2005, 2017
YEAR OF THE ROOSTER
The Rooster is attractive, aggressive, alert and a perfectionist.
Best love match: Ox, Dragon or Snake
Famous Roosters: Britney Spears, Justin Timberlake, Jennifer Aniston, Elton John

1958, 1970, 1982, 1994, 2006, 2018
YEAR OF THE DOG
The Dog is honest, conservative, sympathetic and loyal.

Best love match: Tiger or Horse
Famous Dogs: Madonna, Prince William, Jennifer Lopez, Uma Thurman

1959, 1971, 1983, 1995, 2007, 2019
YEAR OF THE PIG
The Pig is popular, caring, industrious and home-loving.
Best love match: Rabbit/Hare or Sheep/Goat
Famous Pigs: Luke Wilson, Julie Andrews, Stephen King, Ewan McGregor

Mia:	Chinese New Year is so cool! I wish I could celebrate it!
Ling Su:	You can! Draw or find a picture of a dragon, attach it to your coat and go!
Mia:	And don't forget to light your firecrackers WELL AWAY from your face!

X. Conclusion

Are You Listening?

A Note from Her Royal Highness Princess Mia Thermopolis

As you can see, the winter holiday season is just JAM-PACKED with history, tradition and festivities. Who knew the origin of the dreidel was from medieval England, or that St Nicholas's bones once got stolen, or that people used to 'Deck the Halls with Boughs of Holly' in order to look pagan in front of Roman soldiers? Not me.

Personally, I'm glad I learned all this stuff. Because now when I travel to foreign lands – or even just down to Chinatown – I will actually have some idea what people are talking about when they mention mumming or even the Julnisse.

More importantly, however, I'll know that holidays like Christmas, New Year's, Hanukkah and Kwanzaa – different as they may seem from one another – all have one thing in common. And no, it's not presents. It's that they all celebrate birth – rebirth of spring, birth of a saviour, birth of hope – and a time of coming together as families and communities to give thanks for that big wheel in the sky rolling towards us once again.

God bless us, everyone.

Now pass me my presents, please.

Mia's Christmas

Tuesday, December 22, noon, royal Genovian bedchamber

OH MY GOD, THEY'RE COMING!!!! HERE!!!! THEY'RE COMING **HERE!!!!** THEY'LL BE HERE **TOMORROW!!!!**

Why am I the only one who CARES???? Grandmere just looked up from her lemon juice and warm water and went, 'Prepare the blue and-gold wing, please,' to Antoine, the major domo.

AND THAT WAS IT.

She is so tied up with planning her Christmas Eve Ball (royalty from all over the world will be descending on Genovia for it), that she can't think of anything else. Not that anybody else in the family even cares about it. Dad even asked why we couldn't just have a quiet family Christmas for a change.

Grandmere looked at him with daggers in her eyes and then said, as she sorted through all the RSVPs she'd got in the mail, 'Well, if Prince Nikolaos of Greece thinks we're going to put up his polo pony while he's here, he is sadly mistaken.'

My dad just sighed and went back to reading the *Wall Street Journal*.

I am telling you, there is something WRONG with my family.

'Hello? That's *it*?' I cried. 'The future Prince Michael Moscovitz Renaldo is arriving tomorrow for his first visit ever to the country over which he will one day help me rule, and all you can say is "Prepare the blue-and-gold wing" to Antoine?'

That got my dad to look out from behind his newspaper.

'You two are engaged?' There was this total crease in the middle of his forehead. Funny how

I've never noticed it before. If I stuck a penny in there, I bet a gumball would fall out of his mouth. 'When did this happen?'

Sadly I was forced to admit that Michael had not, as yet, proposed.

But it's sure to happen eventually, as a love like the one Michael and I share can never be denied – no matter what the studios who make all those movies allegedly based on my life might think.

'Oh,' my dad said. And lost all interest. The crease completely disappeared. In fact his whole head disappeared, back behind the newspaper.

'Freshly cut flowers will be placed in all the rooms in the blue-and-gold wing, Amelia,' Grandmere said as she banged on the end of her soft-boiled egg with a silver spoon. 'What more do you want? A gala in the young man's honour? As if we don't have enough to worry about with the Christmas Ball. Why must you

171

obsess so over such inconsequential things?'

Inconsequential? INCONSEQUENTIAL? Michael and Lilly's first-ever visit to Genovia is INCONSEQUENTIAL? I mean, sure, they're only coming for a week...a mere seven days ... only 168 hours ...

But I'm trying to stay positive, like Dr Phil says to.

'A week isn't very long to enjoy all the incredible sights this country has to offer.'

That's what Philomena, my dad's latest girlfriend, had to offer to the breakfast convo. Like this wasn't a completely transparent attempt to get in good with my dad. You know, on account of her appreciating his native land so much. Like he was going to throw down his paper and be all, 'Philomena, light of my heart, be mine forever!', because she said you couldn't see everything there is to see in his principality in seven days.

Whatever.

Not that I don't wholly support a woman's right to use her god-given assets to get a prince to propose to her, or to make a career out of strutting down a runway in a thong with a pair of wings attached to the straps of her bra.

I just, you know, hope she's socking some of it away in a decent 401K or some Roth IRAs.

Grandmere ignored Philomena. This is her - custom where my dad's girlfriends are concerned.

'You must be sure to remind Antoine to secure a tuxedo for your young man,' is all Grandmere said. 'I don't want him turning up at the ball in dungarees. And tell Lilly I expect her to have removed all of those horrid "friend-ship" bracelets she wears. Straggly pieces of dirt-collecting yarn, is what I call them. I won't have the Contessa Trevanni thinking my grand-daughter's best friend is a bag lady.'

The whole time she was talking, Rommel, Grandmere's hairless miniature poodle, was totally looking on, so hoping she might drop a crumb or two of the toast she was smearing with soft-boiled egg guts. Because Rommel is on this diet where all he's allowed to eat is specially formulated dog food. This is on account of the royal vet recently diagnosing him with irritable bowel syndrome. Apparently, the IBS is caused by the antidepressants Rommel is taking to combat his OCD, which manifests itself in his licking all of his fur off.

'And the parents of your little friends don't mind them spending Christmas away from home?' Philomena asked, all sweetly.

'No,' I explained to her, speaking slowly because she's Danish. And a model. 'The Moscovitzes don't celebrate Christmas. They're Jewish.'

'And they are coming on the royal Genovian jet?' Philomena asked, her perfectly plucked eyebrows raised. Because she'd had to fly commercial to get to the palace – first class, but still – on account of the jet having been sent to pick up Michael and Lilly.

'A certain person,' my dad said, from behind the paper, 'refused to spend the holidays in Genovia on the grounds that she'd miss her baby brother's first Christmas unless certain demands were met.'

Philomena looked confused, apparently not realizing my dad was talking about me and the temper tantrum that had finally forced him to send the jet for Lilly and Michael.

'But that's terrible,' Philomena said in her Danish accent. 'Who would rather stay in America for the holidays than come to this beautiful place?'

Really, I don't know how I'm supposed to endure the anti-Americanism that is just rampant in this part of the world. Sometimes it just makes my blood boil.

But whatever.

THEY'RE COMING!!!! They'll be here in twenty-four hours!!!! I have to get to work if I'm going to have everything ready for them in time.

TO DO LIST

1. Make sure Michael gets the Prince Guillaume royal memorial bedchamber, the one with the panoramic view of the Genovian bay – and not just because its balcony is right next to mine and we can sneak out at night and climb over each other's railings and watch the moon rise while we're in one another's arms. Michael! My love! It's been three whole days since last we met!

2. Have Antoine put the good guest soaps in their rooms, and not the cruddy soap made

from Genovian olive oil with the royal crest printed on it, which never foams up.

3. Make sure the palace kitchen has Heinz ketchup because that's the only kind Lilly likes.

4. MAKE SURE SATELLITE TV IS HOOKED UP IN ALL BEDROOMS!

5. Find out what is up with my hair.

6. Make sure there are plenty of copies of smart magazines like *The New Yorker* and *Time* lying around, not just *US Weekly* and *CosmoGirl*. Don't want Michael assuming all I think about is celebrities and my appearance!

7. Crest Whitestrips. Get them. Use them.

8. Cuticles. I have totally let them go. And now they're all gross and bloody-looking. Just the kind of look a girl wants for her hands, when she hasn't seen her boyfriend in three days.

9. TOENAILS!!!! CUT THEM!!!! I'm starting to look like one of those rhesus monkeys.

10. Double check Christmas shopping list:
Dad – Subscription to *Golf Digest*. Done.✓
Grandmere – Padded satin hangers, as per usual. She herself said a princess can never have too many. Done.✓
Philomena – What DOES the modern princess get for her dad's latest skank? I'm thinking Pussy Pucker Pots vegan lip balm, so at least Dad won't be ingesting harmful animal by-products every time he sticks his tongue in her mouth. Done.✓
Mom – Yoga pants. Not that she does yoga. But she loves anything with elastic waistbands at this point in her battle to lose her leftover pregnancy weight. Done.✓
Mr G – Bose headphones so we don't have to listen to his AC/DC. Done.✓

Rocky – Baby Mozart video, since research suggests that a relationship exists between exposure to Mozart's music and increases in spatial-reasoning abilities and intelligence, and I don't want Rocky to suffer the way I am when HE gets to Geometry. Done.✓

Fat Louie – Catnip in a sock. He's not picky. Done.✓

Lars – Renew his subscription to *Guns & Ammo*. Done.✓

Tina – Book on how to write a romance novel and get it published. Done.✓

Ling Su – Paintbrushes . . . NOT ones made out of animal fur. Done.✓

Shameeka – All the episodes of *The OC* I secretly taped for her, since she isn't allowed to watch that show. Done.✓

Boris – Copy of *Queer Eye for the Straight Guy's Guide to Dressing Better*. Done.✓

Lilly – Copy of *If I'm So Wonderful, Why Am I Still Single? Ten Strategies That Will Change Your Love Life Forever*. Done.✓

It is very hard to figure out what to get for Lilly and Michael, because they celebrate Hanukkah and that amounts to EIGHT nights of one present each as opposed to ONE day where you're LUCKY if you get eight presents. And even though Lilly says most of her presents are things like underwear and socks, I can't help feeling like Jewish kids get a way better deal out of their holiday than we do with ours. Although Lilly says it is murder trying to think up eight gifts for her dad, because how many ties and/or magazine subscriptions can you give one person?

Pavlov and Rommel – Might-Y-Bone. Done.✓

Michael – This is the really hard one. I

have to get Michael something totally good for Christmas, because the Hanukkah gift I gave him was such a bust. I guess I should have known, because Dance Dance Revolution Party for PlayStation 2 was something *I* wanted. I just assumed he'd want it too. Well, OK, I knew he wouldn't really want it, but I thought once he saw how FUN it was, he'd want it too. But I can tell he never uses it unless I come over because the floor pad is always exactly the way I folded it the last time.

So now I totally have to come up with something GREAT for Christmas to make up for my Hanukkah GAFFE. So I'm getting him an original single-sided 27 x 41-inch movie poster from the 1977 George Lucas classic *Star Wars,* in near-mint condition, according to the seller on eBay that I'm trying to buy it from. It will look very nice in Michael's dorm room. The bidding is at $23.72, with two days left to go. I put in $50.00 as my top bid. Nobody better bid more than me or I'll be forced to kill myself, on account of how I had to sell my precious Fiesta Giles *Buffy the Vampire Slayer* action figure just to get enough money to be able to afford Michael's gift (which blows because, except for Military Xander, which I was missing, I had the complete set). Plus I only got $28.00 for Giles in his sombrero, so it looks like I'm going to have to dip into my savings.

But that's OK. Michael is soooooo worth it.

Dear Antoine,

I know you are busy preparing the blue-and-gold wing for the Moscovitzes, who will be arriving tomorrow. I just thought I would let you know of a few things you might want to put in each of their rooms to make them feel at home.

Michael Moscovitz:
- Telescope (that really big one from the royal planetarium will do)
- Power Mac G5 with 23-inch Cinema Display and AirPort Extreme Base Station

- CD player and Flaming Lips's 'Yoshimi Battles the Pink Robots'

Lilly Moscovitz:
- Segway Human Transporter
- 'Diagnostic and Statistical Manual of Mental Disorders DSM-V-TR'
- CD player and Lash's 'The Beautiful and the Damned'

Also, mini-fridges in each room filled with Yoo-Hoo and chocolate-covered pretzels for late-night snacking would be very much appreciated.

HRH Mia Thermopolis

Tuesday, December 22, 11 p.m., royal Genovian bedchamber

I perfectly understand my dad objecting to buying a Segway Human Transporter for Lilly. But he didn't have to be so crabby about it. They have totally fixed them so they don't have that problem where they flop over any more.

Also, I think one would be quite handy for, say, reviewing the royal Genovian troops. You would think my dad would appreciate my efforts to get the palace to move into the twenty-first century. But I guess not.

I don't know why Grandmere threw such a fit over my Christmas list either. I think all of the things I asked for were perfectly reasonable.

MIA THERMOPOLIS'S CHRISTMAS WISH LIST

1. World Peace
2. Save the endangered sea turtle
3. iPod and Power Book with $100 gift card to iTunes Online Music Store
4. Re-implementation of the NYC recycling programmes eliminated by mayor
5. TiVo
6. End to world hunger
7. Military Xander *BTVS* action figure
8. Segway Human Transporter
9. Eliminate fossil-fuel emissions contributing to global warming
10. Ab roller, so I can look like Britney Spears

What's wrong with all that, I'd like to know? You can get the ab roller right off the Home Shopping Network. And they sell Segways on amazon.com!

Whatever. Like I don't have bigger stuff to worry about. They'll be here in twelve hours!!!! I went and checked their rooms, and Antoine didn't get them a single thing I asked him to. Instead of the *DSM*, he put a copy of *The History of Genovia* in Lilly's room. And instead of a telescope, he put BINOCULARS in Michael's room (I took them. The last thing I need is for Michael to discover that the German tourists down on the Genovian beach like to sunbathe topless. Like I need that kind of competition!).

And there was no Yoo-Hoo in the mini-fridges. Just Orangina! Like orange soda goes with chocolate-covered pretzels! EW! You would think Antoine had never drunk Sunny D then eaten an Oreo in his life. A taste as disgusting as that can scar the tastebuds forever.

That's not the worst of it though. The worst is that tonight at dinner, Tante Simone was fully asking me if I was going to dance with

Prince William at the Ball, and when I said no, Grandmere went BERSERK. In front of Philomena and Dad and Prince René and Sebastiano (who are here for the holidays) and the footmen and EVERYBODY!!!

Then Tante Jean-Marie got into the act, and started saying all this stuff about how there are a lot of fish in the sea and I shouldn't limit myself at such a young age to one person, especially someone who isn't even of royal blood himself. I don't know where those three even get off – Grandmere and her sisters, I mean. They have their OWN chateau, Miragnac, right down the road. Why don't they ever stay THERE? I mean, I know Grandmere feels like she has to hang around the palace to act as hostess since there is none, but . . .

Oh my God, how am I supposed to concentrate with that hideous noise coming from outside? I understand that people are excited that it's nearly Christmas, but they ought to show some respect for others by not CATER-WAULING underneath other people's royal bedroom balconies . . .

Wednesday, December 23, 1 a.m., royal Genovian bedchamber

It wasn't drunken tourists making all that noise under my balcony after all. It was the sweetest little black-and-white cat! Why can't people take better care of their pets? I swear she must have been starving. When I left, she was still chowing on the two pounds of leftover lobster thermidor I stole from the royal kitchen for her. But she'd already managed to put away most of the caviar.

Anyway, let's see, where was I?

Oh yes. My totally embarrassing family. I swear, if any of them says anything about how I should dance with Prince William while Michael is here, I am fully going *Chasing Liberty* on them.

Ten hours until they get here! I have GOT to get some sleep or I'll have puffy eyes AND a giant zit tomorrow. I found one on my chin just now. Although I globbed a pile of toothpaste on it so hopefully it will be gone by morning.

Wednesday, December 23, noon, royal palace toilette

They're here!!!!

Oh my God, it was SO WEIRD to see Lilly and Michael with, like, palm trees and the ocean in the background. They got out of the limo, all blinking from the bright Mediterranean sunlight and stuff, and I rushed up and was all, 'Welcome to Genovia!', and they looked around at the royal guard standing at arms by the palace doors and all the tourists pressed up against the gates they'd just driven through, snapping photos and going, 'There she is! The Princess of Genovia! Mort, get a picture!'

And Lilly went, 'You LIVE here? It's bigger than the freaking Met,' which is, you know, an understandable reaction, I guess. I mean, she's only seen photos of the palace before. It IS sort of overwhelming when you find out there are thirty-two bedrooms, a ballroom, two pools (outdoor and indoor), a home theatre and a bowling alley (Grandpere routinely scored in the high two-hundreds).

And when Franco, the footman, came up and tried to take Lilly's Emily Rocks! DJ bag from her, she snatched it back and was like, 'Dude, that's MINE.'

But then I gently explained that Franco was a royal footman and that he gets paid to help carry palace guests' stuff.

So then Lilly got all excited and gave Franco her wheelie bag and her Diskman and her pea coat and her royal Genovian jet sleeping mask and her Dr Martens, which she'd been wearing around her neck, since they wouldn't fit into her bag and she'd worn her moon boots for comfort on the transatlantic flight.

All Michael did was grab and kiss me. Which you can bet plenty of tourists got snaps of. I heard them all going, 'Quick! Did you get that? We can make a fortune selling it to the *Enquirer*!' as their digital cameras clicked away.

So now Lilly and Michael are 'freshening up', because that's what Grandmere makes every single overnight guest who arrives at the palace do as soon as they get here. I showed them to their rooms myself (well, Franco followed, along with Antoine, who was all worried about the Yoo-Hoo slip-up) and I'm glad to say my fears were for nothing. They both seemed perfectly happy with the rooms they'd been assigned . . . especially Michael, when I pointed out the thing about our balconies being right next door to each other.

After they're 'freshened', Antoine's supposed to take them on a tour of the palace while I do a quick photo-op with Dad and Grandmere and the Fabergé Advent calendar in the Hall of Mirrors.

But after that, we can hang all day.

Well, until I have to go light the Christmas tree in the Genovian town square.

But then we can do whatever we want!!!!

Um, until dinner anyway. Some of the guests for tomorrow night's Ball have already started arriving, and I promised Dad and Grandmere I'd help entertain the younger royals.

But then after that, we'll be free for fun for sure!!!!

Wednesday, December 23, 11 p.m., royal Genovian bedchamber

Disaster.

First of all, I don't know what's wrong with Lilly. I mean, I KNOW that the palace is filled with riches that, if sold, could feed hundreds of thousands of starving people. The Fabergé Advent calendar alone – being an exact replica of the Genovian palace, only in Fabergé's version, each shuttered window can be opened to reveal a perfectly cut jewel, one for every day of Advent – is insured for seventeen million dollars.

But hello. The Fabergé Advent calendar is not MINE. The da Vinci sketches in the Gallerie aren't mine either. I do not own the Rembrandts in the Grand Hall or the Rodin in the royal garden or even the Monet hanging over the bath-tub in my own royal bathing chamber.

Yet.

And until I do own them, I can't sell them and donate the money to Oxfam or Human Rights Watch, the way Lilly seems to think I should.

And what was all that about the gross materialism of Christmas while we were at the tree lighting? Hello. All I did was plug in the tree in the middle of the town square while everybody stood around clapping. Is it my fault that after the ceremony they all went back to the baccarat tables? Tourism is responsible for a very significant portion of Genovia's econ-omy, and a big draw for the tourists is gambling.

And Genovia uses a lot of that money to help the poor, as I pointed out to Lilly on our way back to the palace. Hello, we don't even make our citizens pay TAXES.

But Lilly just went on making rude remarks, until even Michael, who is the most even-tempered of men, finally turned around and was like, 'Lilly. Shut *up*.'

Of course she didn't listen to him. And I knew it was only going to get worse when, after we all went to change for dinner, Lilly showed up in the Crystal Pavilion where we'd gathered for pre-meal kir royales wearing her WWJJD (What Would Joan Jett Do?) T-shirt and a pair of low-rise jeans that I happen to know for a fact her mom expressly forbade her to wear in public. I practically had to throw myself on her to keep Grandmere from spying them and having a cocktail-hour embolism.

'Lilly,' I hissed, 'what are you doing in that? I told you, dinner here is a very formal affair.'

'Oh, what,' Lilly said, looking disgusted. 'You want me to dress like that hoser over there?' She pointed at Camilla Parker-Bowles. 'Yeah, because pink taffeta so suits my personality.'

'No,' I said. 'But you could at least show some respect for my dad, who went to all the trouble of sending the jet for you and is putting you up for a week. I mean, you think Michael is happy wearing that suit?'

We both looked over at Michael, who was tugging at his shirt collar while having a very in-depth conversation about cyclotron frequency with Prince Andrew. Uncomfortable in his suit as Michael clearly was, he still looked totally hot.

'See?' I glared at Lilly. 'Your brother knows enough not to insult his host. Why don't you?'

Lilly rolled her eyes.

'Fine,' she said. 'I'll change. But you gotta show me how to get back to my room. This place is so huge, I took a wrong turn and ended up in some bowling alley . . .'

I looked around and saw Franco passing by with a tray of canapés. I signalled to him, and he came right over and said he'd be only too happy to show Miss Moscovitz back to her room. So the two of them left . . . for an extraordinarily long time actually.

But by the time Lilly got back (just before Antoine came out and announced that dinner was served), she'd changed into a Betsey Johnson number that at least didn't have any writing on it, so I thought everything would be all right.

Yeah. Right.

I don't know whose idea it was to seat Lilly between my cousins René and Pierre, the thirteen-year-old Comte de Brissac. All I know is that midway through the soup course, René threw down his napkin, got up and stormed off, muttering French swear words and saying something about how it was the fascists who drove his family from their ancestral Italian palace, not inbreeding as Lilly had apparently suggested. He didn't come back until dessert, and even then he took a seat at the far end of the table, vacated by one elderly duke with an apparent incontinence problem, and sat scowling into his blancmange.

Pierre, however, didn't seem to have a problem with Lilly. In fact, he stared at her throughout the seven-course meal in a manner reminiscent of the way Seth stared at Summer in the early episodes of *The OC*.

But attacking my family members was apparently not enough for Lilly. She had to start in on Philomena next . . .

. . . which really, if you think about it, is totally beneath her. I mean, for someone of Lilly's abilities – and she scored a 210 on an online IQ test we took together earlier in the year; I only got a 120 (although on the EMOTIONAL IQ test I got a 120, and she only got a 90) – goading Philomena is like shooting rubber bands at rats on the subway tracks.

'So, Philo,' Lilly began conversationally. 'You meet a lot of princes in your line of work?'

Philomena smiled and went, 'Oh, no, not so many.'

'So when you finally do meet one, you really have to hang on to him,' Lilly said in a this-is-just-between-us-girls tone.

'Oh, well,' Philomena said with a laugh, glancing at my dad to see if he was listening – he wasn't. He was talking to King Juan Carlos of Spain about golf. 'Yes, of course.'

'Because,' Lilly went on in the same conspiratorial manner, 'seeing as how you make your living on your looks and never bothered to pursue any kind of higher educa- tion, as soon as your boobs start to sag your modelling agency will kick you out on your butt and you won't have two euros to rub together, will you? So you'd better marry a prince – or a rock star – pronto or it's buh-bye those four-hundred-dollar highlights, right?'

'Lilly,' I said, starting to get up, 'can I have a word with you in the salon?'

'No need,' Lilly said with a dazzling smile. 'Oh, look. The cheese course.'

Fortunately Philomena lacked a firm enough grasp of the English language – or was simply too dumb – to have understood what Lilly was saying to her. She just smiled and looked confused, her usual expression.

Pierre, however, looked totally impressed. I even heard him murmur, over his St Andre triple-cream cheese, 'Mademoiselle, you intoxicate me.'

To which Lilly replied, 'You have Roquefort on your cravat, kid.'

As if all that wasn't bad enough, after dinner, when the adults went into the salon for cigars and port and gossip, and I was left to entertain the younger royals with Fanta, some spoons and a deck of cards, Lilly looked around, yawned and said, 'Jet lag. Going to bed. See you tomorrow,' and vanished!

Michael and I were forced to play Spoon for **TWO HOURS** with Pierre and a bunch of other under-twenty-one royals . . . who, by the way, weren't very impressed with the game. Lord Mulberry, Princes William and Harry's second cousin, kept asking why we couldn't play strip poker instead.

You know, you would have thought that all of us royals would get along much better, considering each and every one of us (well, except Michael) has the weight of a throne resting upon our teenage shoulders, and several of us know what it's like to have movies made about our lives . . . movies that aren't exactly strictly FACTUAL, if you know what I mean, and take a certain number of **LIBERTIES** with the truth.

I don't know how Michael managed to stay

awake, having just come from another time zone and all. I know MY eyes were drooping and I'd had three days to get used to Genovian time already. I barely even managed to kiss him goodnight before stumbling into my room and into bed.

As if all of that isn't bad enough, someone topped my $50.00 bid on Michael's *Star Wars* poster! With only twelve hours left on the bidding, I put in a high bid of $75.00. With expedited shipping to get it here by Christmas, I am only just barely going to be able—

Oh my God. What is that? Someone is at my balcony door!

Oooooh. Not someone. *Michael.*

Suddenly I don't feel so sleepy any more . . .

Thursday, December 24, 1 a.m., royal Genovian bedchamber

Oh my God, I can't *believe* what just happened! Michael and I were having a lovely time making out on my balcony under the stars, with the scent of bougainvillea filling our nostrils, and the glow of the Christmas tree downtown just enough for us to see by, when suddenly we were interrupted by the most unearthly wail . . . I swear, I thought the ghost of Prince Guillaume, in whose memorial bedchamber Michael is supposed to be sleeping, had come back to get all in my face about kissing a non-royal—

Only it turned out it wasn't the ghost of Prince Guillaume. It was that little black-and-white cat again!

Only this time she'd brought a friend! Not just one, it turned out. But five. Five little starving friends!

Michael was against feeding them. He said that would just make them come around more often. But what was I supposed to do, let them starve before my eyes?

Michael said they didn't look too starved to him and pointed out – after I'd dragged him down to the garden to see how cute they were for himself – that they all seemed well within normal weight, and that one was even wearing a collar.

But I know from having seen so many episodes of *Miracle Pets* that just because a cat is wearing a collar doesn't mean it isn't starving or a long, long way from home. For instance, one couple lost their cat when it climbed into a neighbour's removal van. They didn't see it again for three months, when they received a call from a fur trapper in Alaska, 3,000 miles away, who said he'd found their cat in a tree outside his cabin and did they want it back?

So we snuck into the royal kitchens and scraped up some leftover Crown roast and fillet of sole to feed the poor starving things.

And you could tell they were really grateful because the hum of their mutual purr as they chowed down was almost as loud as the beat of waves down on the beach below.

After all of that, of course, Michael could fight his jet lag no longer, not even for kissing.

But that's all right, because there's always tomorrow night!!!! The best Christmas present I could ever ask for would be another night of kissing with Michael under the Genovian night sky.

One weird thing though: when Michael and I were coming back upstairs from feeding the cats, I thought I saw Franco, the footman, leaving the blue-and-gold wing, looking kind of . . . flushed.

I wonder what he could have been doing there?

Oh well, maybe Lilly woke up in the middle of the night and needed an egg cream or something. I'll ask her in the morning.

I can't believe Michael is sleeping in the room RIGHT NEXT DOOR to mine. Only a single wall – and a bathroom with a jacuzzi tub and all of the plumbing to operate it – separates us! Goodnight, my cherished preserver! Sleep well!

Oh my gosh, I hope that if I snore he doesn't hear me through the wall.

Thursday, December 24, 5 p.m., royal Genovian bedchamber

A MUCH better day than yesterday so far. Actually one of the best days I've ever spent in Genovia!

For one thing, I WON THE *STAR WARS* POSTER!!!! Yes!!! I was the highest bidder!!! I have already contacted the seller and he agreed to airline express it so it arrives in time for Christmas tomorrow.

YES!!!! She shoots, she scores.

As if that wasn't good enough, Lilly was actually in a good mood today. She was laughing and joking from breakfast on. It was like she'd turned, overnight, into a different person. She didn't go out of her way to antagonize Grandmere or even Prince René (who nevertheless gave her a wide berth, announcing that he was going clay-pigeon shooting with Mrs Parker-Bowles and the Prince of Wales, and not returning to the palace until teatime). She didn't say a word about the seven pounds of kippers at the breakfast buffet, and even seemed to have fun dipping slivers of buttered toast into her first ever soft-boiled egg.

Then the truly miraculous thing occurred: Grandmere – who was bustling around with a walkie-talkie, barking orders at Antoine as more and more royals (Crown Princess Mathilde of Belgium's glider almost landed on the conservatory) poured in from all over Europe and beyond – commanded us to leave the palace. Grandmere said she was tired of having so many children underfoot. And so she'd ordered the royal yacht to take us on a cruise up and down the Genovian coast for the rest of the day!

And OK, we had to take the other teenage – and younger – royals with us.

But still! A day at sea, instead of hanging around, shaking the gifts under the twenty-foot-tall Christmas tree in the Great Hall and concluding that none of them was big enough to be a Segway, and being forced to stand around at boring holiday events like the hideous rite of the olive branch, in which the youngest member of the family (namely, me) has to take an olive-oil-soaked branch and poke it around in the fireplace while muttering stuff about wishing the family health and happiness for the coming year, while everybody else gets to swig grappa, aka hard liquor, made from the grapes left over after pressing.

Um, hello. I'll take the day at sea.

You can see why I fought so hard to stay in New York for the holidays. My mom and Mr G's only holiday tradition includes decorating a tree with cut-out portraits of famous people who died during the previous year, and then ordering in Peking duck from Number One Noodle Son and eating it while watching *A Christmas Story* for the nine millionth time. Heaven.

Anyway, we all went to change into our maritime clothes (jeans and a sweater for Michael; khakis and a windbreaker for me; overalls and a shirt that said *ToughTitties* for Lilly – but it was OK because the overall bib hid it; chinos, a navy-blue blazer and a red-and-gold tie for Pierre, Princes William and Harry, Lord Mulberry and the other male royals; Lily Pulitzer everything for the Princesses of York and the females on the Grimaldi side of the family, who by the way are still pretending we aren't related).

I wanted to bring Princess Aiko of Japan along SO badly (she is officially the cutest royal I have ever seen), but her mom wouldn't let me, even when I explained that, having a very young sibling myself back home for which I am often sole caretaker, Rocky's father being, you know, a man, and my mother being an anarchist, I am probably the most responsible royal on the planet to leave a toddler with.

But Princess Masako totally didn't go for it. Bummer.

Once we got down to the pier where the boat was waiting, I passed out non-drowsiness-formula Dramamine to anyone who wanted some (Michael and Lilly took me up on the offer, but none of the royals did. Some of the Windsors, who shall remain nameless, even sneered at me. Gosh, I'm sorry. Just because you've spent every holiday of your life on a yacht or a set of skis, don't scoff at those of us who haven't. I'd like to see you figure out how to get from Fourteenth and Ninth Avenue all the way to Seventy-seventh and Lex with a single swipe of your MetroCard. Ha! Bet you don't feel so cocky now, do you, Your High and Mightynesses?).

Captain Marco had us out of the Genovian harbour – past all of the smaller yachts belonging to the German tourists as well as the colossally huge cruise ship that had pulled in so its passengers could spend Christmas Eve in Genovia – and at sea in no time. It was really beautiful once we were skimming along the deep-blue water, the wind in our hair and the sun in our faces.

It was too cold to swim, of course, but it got quite toasty sitting in the sun, swilling down Orangina and nibbling shrimp cocktail. So toasty, in fact, that some of the boys had to remove their blazers. I kept a close watch on Michael and was totally rewarded for my efforts by catching an eyeful of naked chest when he finally pulled his sweater off. Because part of his T-shirt came off with it, before he had a chance to tug it down again.

In all, a *very* lovely day.

There was a BIT of weirdness when I went over to Lilly's deckchair to ask her if she wanted any caprese salad and I saw Lord Mulberry sitting beside her. Their heads – her dark one and his blond one – were kind of close together.

Which is odd because Lilly is virulently opposed to the British monarchy. The idea of taxation to support an unelected head of state offends her, and she says she eagerly awaits the downfall of England's aristocracy (she says Genovia is OK because we don't tax our citizens . . . which is why so many people want to move here).

Still, somehow it didn't look to me as if Lilly was sharing this opinion with Lord Mulberry, who happens to be about twenty-fifth in line to the British throne. Especially since, when I walked up to them, he was laughing at something she'd said as if it were the most hilarious joke he had ever heard.

When he saw me, though, he clammed up and went, 'There's a man I've got to see about a dog.' Then he moved to the front of the boat. Even though I happen to know the only people up there were some of my Grimaldi cousins, who are allergic to dogs. Or at least that's what they say to Grandmere whenever she asks them to dogsit for Rommel.

But when I asked Lilly what that had been all about, she said she and Lord Mulberry had just been discussing the weather.

When I walked away, though, the Comte de Brissac sprang out from behind a lifeboat and informed me in a low voice that the young lord had been 'pestering Mademoiselle Moscovitz' all day long.

. . . and that, as if that were not enough, Franco the Footman had come by so often to ask Lilly if she needed anything, such as foot rubs or the *Herald Tribune*, that he (Pierre) believed Franco was 'taking liberties' and would have liked to have seen 'that hireling flogged for his overfamiliarity with the young lady'.

To which the only sane reply was, 'You are one weird little dude, Pierre.'

But the Comte totally took it as a compliment. He bowed and went, 'I feel it my duty to watch out for the fairer sex at all times.'

So then I went back to Lilly's deckchair and asked her if Lord Mulberry was bothering her and if Franco had been overly familiar.

Lilly tilted her sunglasses so she could see me properly and went, 'Huh?'

So I explained what the Comte had said he'd seen and Lilly snorted, lowered her sunglasses again and said, 'That little French weasel. Franco's just doing his job. And Lord Mulberry was only putting sunscreen on the backs of my calves where I couldn't reach.' I noticed that she'd rolled up the legs of her overalls. 'He was being quite helpful.'

'Oh,' I said. 'Well . . . I guess that's all right then.'

But when I went to report this to Pierre, he only laughed cynically and said, 'Have you ever had a problem reaching the backs of your calves by yourself, *Princesse*? I myself have not.'

Hmmm. I think maybe Lilly is starting to like the lifestyle of the rich and royal a little *too* much.

Still. It was a nice day. No one got pushed into the water and one of the Princesses of York even caught a fish!

Now we all have to get changed for the Ball. I already checked Lilly's wardrobe and she has a totally nice black satin and tulle number with a pink ribbon to wear (thank God Dr Moscovitz insisted on a trip to Neiman Marcus before putting Lilly on the plane). Grandmere ought to have no complaints.

And I happened to catch a glimpse of Michael just now through his balcony doors (I was NOT spying. I had to go out on the balcony to see whether or not it was chilly enough for the satin stole that came with my dress) in his tux, and all I can say is . . . move over, Orlando Bloom.

Thursday, December 24, 11.30 p.m., royal Genovian bedchamber

I don't care what Grandmere says. I did NOT ruin her ball. I DIDN'T.

Lilly did.

Well, it was MOSTLY Lilly anyway. I'll admit she had a bit of help.

Everything was going fine until they made me dance with Prince William. How was I supposed to keep an eye on Lilly when I was so nervous that my boyfriend might, at any moment, grab the second in line to the throne of England in a fit of jealous rage and break his nose? Not that Michael even appeared to NOTICE that I was dancing with someone else, so absorbed was he in his conversation with Prince Carl Philip of Sweden on the role of enzymes and gene-regulatory elements in bio-technology and genetic engineering.

Still, a girl can dream.

Anyway, in my disappointment that Michael was not in the least bit jealous over my dancing with the most eligible bachelor in the world, I forgot to watch what Lilly was doing . . .

And that's when Pierre came running into the middle of the ballroom – his tuxedo tails flying behind him like a cape – slid to a halt in his patent-leather dancing slippers and screamed, 'Stop them! Somebody stop them!'

Of course Grandmere immediately assumed someone was trying to steal the Fabergé Advent calendar. She tore herself from the arms of the guy she'd been dancing with – who turned out to have been Prince Hashem of Jordan – and charged after the Comte, shrieking, 'Not the Fabergé! Anything but the Fabergé!'

But when we all dashed after him we found

the Comte headed towards the bowling alley, not the Hall of Mirrors.

And it was in that bowling alley that we were met by the most horrifying sight I personally have ever witnessed:

Lilly, with about seven or eight of the young royals – whose identity I dare not record even in my own diary in case the paparazzi someday get their hands on it – engaged in a game of what can only be described as . . .

Strip bowling.

As if seeing Lilly making a strike in her Hello Kitty underwear wasn't bad enough, we were even more flabbergasted to see an enraged Franco throw down the tray of canapés he'd been carrying and challenge Lord Mulberry (who'd been keeping score in nothing but a pair of tighty-whities) to a duel over Lilly's honour!

The effect of this sight on the Ball attendees was electrifying to say the least. Prince René grinned and strode forward as if he were about to join in on the game – until my dad put a restraining hand on his shoulder, that is. The Contessa Trevanni gasped and threw her hands over her granddaughter's eyes, to shield her from the shocking sight. Prince Charles's ears turned as red as a pair of traffic stop lights. Princes William and Harry immediately started snapping photos with their cellphone cameras, apparently with the intent of blackmailing their second cousin at a later date. The young Comte pointed at Lilly and cried in anguished tones, 'I'd have treated you like a queen . . . but I won't be your bitch!'

Lord Mulberry told Franco that he had no intention of fighting anybody, at which point Franco stripped off one of his white gloves and slapped the lord across the face with it . . . in direct violation of royal Genovian footman guidelines.

At which point Prince René immediately began going around taking bets on the outcome of the fight, as a second later, Lord Mulberry's fist connected with Franco's gut. The poor little Comte had to be physically held back – who knew Princess Anne was so strong? – to be kept from throwing himself into the fight as well.

I think it might have been all right in the end if the two fighters hadn't tumbled through the doors to the bowling alley and then into the Hall of Mirrors . . .

'NOT THE FABERGÉ,' screamed Grandmere.

But it was too late. A second later, the brawling men rolled into the table holding the Fabergé Advent calendar, sending it crashing to the floor.

At which point Grandmere fainted dead away.

Thank God Michael and Prince Philip were standing near enough to catch her.

'We need to get her some air,' Michael said in a commanding tone. Really, he is so good in a crisis. It's kind of thrilling to watch. 'Out of the way!'

Everyone's bodyguards scurried to make room while Michael and Prince Philip – with the help of my dad – carried Grandmere towards the nearest set of French doors, which happened to lead out into the garden . . .

. . . the same garden in which I'd discovered that poor little black-and-white cat.

Only instead of only bringing by four or five of her friends, tonight she'd brought about seven or eight . . .

Dozen.

The entire garden was filled with crying cats. White cats. Grey cats. Calico cats. Fat cats. Thin cats. Cats draped in trees. Cats lounging on the side of the fountain. Cats sitting on top of the stone wall. More cats than I had ever seen in one place in my whole life.

And all of them miaowing for more lobster thermidor.

Everyone stood staring at the cats in stunned silence until one of them – the little black-and-white cat I'd befriended in the first place – came sauntering up and started rubbing her head against my legs, through the silky satin of my evening gown.

At which point Grandmere raised her head, opened her eyes, took in the scene with a disbelieving look on her face then glanced towards me and screamed, 'MIA!!!!'

Well. At least for once she remembered to call me by my real name.

Too tired to write. More later.

Friday, December 25, 8 a.m.,
royal Genovian bedchamber

It's Christmas. But I don't see anything too merry about it.

Last night was a total debacle. Between the naked royals – not to mention Lilly – the fight between Lord Mulberry and Franco (sadly for René, a winner could not immediately be determined, as the fracas was broken up too quickly by the Royal Genovian Guard), the Advent calendar (apparently it can be salvaged . . . but not in time for use for next year) and the cats, Grandmere's Christmas Eve Ball will probably go down in history as Genovia's most disastrous party of all time.

I can't even sleep any more because the sound of all the car doors being slammed by indignant royals getting into their Rolls-Royces and being driven away keeps waking me up. Most of them – according to Jeanette, one of the maids, who just came in with a cup of hot chocolate for me – are claiming to have allergies to cat dander.

But you so know a big part of why they're leaving is that they want to keep their kids away from Lilly's bad influence. Even the Prince and Princess of Japan, and THEIR kid is only four or whatever.

Though to be fair, some of those teen royals . . . let's just say I highly doubt this is the first time most of them – particularly those Grimaldis – have ever participated in a game of strip bowling.

Oh, well. At least now my dad will have the quiet Christmas he wanted in the first place.

I guess I should get dressed and go see what's going on downstairs. I know it can't be good.

Friday, December 25, 11 a.m., royal Genovian Great Hall

Well, the gift-giving has begun.

Dad really seemed to like his subscription to *Golf Digest*. And even Grandmere couldn't help looking pleased at her padded satin hangers. She kept a pretty stiff upper lip all through breakfast and church, not mentioning a word about what happened last night, even when Lilly showed up at the table in the sweats she wears as pyjamas. At least she'd put on the Genovian Palace terry-cloth robe Antoine had hung in all the guest rooms.

It looked kind of funny with her moon boots though.

I expected Lilly to apologize – not to me, but to Grandmere at least. Instead she just reached for some toast and started buttering it. I guess she's still upset about my dad firing Franco for striking a royal.

But, really, it's not like my dad had any choice. I mean, Prince Charles might very well have pressed charges. He didn't, thank God. But he COULD have. He settled instead for dragging a besotted Lord Mulberry off to Las Vegas for the weekend with the Princes William and Harry, in the hopes that a run-in with Paris Hilton would cause him to forget about his passion for Lilly.

Lilly, for her part, argued that Franco had been rendered temporarily insane by his passion for her, and that it was wrong to deprive a man of his livelihood for momentarily letting his id get the better of him.

But Franco, with surprising dignity, told her that he didn't need her to fight his battles for him. Then he turned his footman livery over to

Antoine and strode from the palace forever.

Lilly wept and said she and Franco had a relationship that was stronger than mere friendship or love. But since she'd said the exact same thing about a busboy just last year – not to mention Lord Mulberry, just the night before – I can't say I was too impressed.

I noticed Michael didn't look impressed either. He studiously ignored his sister all through breakfast, so I did the same. Although it was kind of hard since it was just Michael, Lilly, Dad, Tantes Simone and Jean-Marie, and Grandmere and me at the table. Philomena was still in bed, claiming to have a migraine (which might actually have been the smartest thing she's ever done); Prince René had run off with the Contessa Trevanni's granddaughter, much to the Contessa's delight; and Sebastiano had crept away in the early hours with Prince Albert, leaving behind a breakfast table set for a hundred and enough bacon to clog the arteries of the entire population of Bulgaria.

After church Grandmere announced that the gift exchange was to proceed, so we're sitting here opening packages. Back home in New York we just open all the presents at the same time and are done in ten minutes. Here in Genovia Grandmere likes to go around in a circle, having each person open one present, then show it to everyone and thank the giver personally. It takes HOURS.

Here is what I have got so far:

- Dolce and Gabbana pink cashmere leg warmers (from Philomena).
- Ballerina music box from Tante Simone (who persists in thinking I am still nine years old).
- Hand-crocheted muffler from Tante Jean-Marie. Because, you know, it gets so cold in

Genovia (median year-round temperature 70 degrees).

- Copy of *America's Queen: The Life of Jacqueline Kennedy Onassis* from Sebastiano, who considers Jackie O the epitome of beaut (beauty) after Prin Di (Princess Diana).

- An electric razor from Paolo (very funny. Not.).

- The Princess Mia Madame Alexander doll from Mamaw and Papaw (um, who apparently did not get the message that I am not particularly enthused over the fact that someone made a doll of me, let alone the psychotic look in this doll's eyes, or the fact that she is wearing overalls with a tiara and has this stupid banner that says *Save the Whales* on it).

- Both of the movies they have made of my life so far on DVD from Prince René (again, very funny. Not.).

- A new tiara from Grandmere. Because, you know, no princess should be without a pair of tiaras; in case one tiara is no longer able to perform its duties, then the back-up tiara can be called upon to fill in.

*

So far, I've only got one thing I asked for . . . an iBook with an iPod from Mom and Dad and a gift certificate to iTunes from Mr G. At least now I won't be the only person in the entire Tri-State area who hasn't gone Mac yet. It doesn't look like I'm going to end up getting Military Xander or world peace or anything else on my list, but that's OK, I guess. I'm pretty much used to disappointment at this point in my life.

My present for Michael showed up by special delivery while we were at church. I had to pay as much for shipping as I did for the actual present to get it here on time, but I know it will be totally worth it when he opens it and freaks out over its incredible rarity and coolness.

Oh, it's Lilly's turn. She's opening my present to her. I kind of wish now that I'd given her something else. I mean, since she doesn't seem to have any trouble finding romantic partners these days.

Ooops. Lilly doesn't look very happy . . .

Friday, December 25, noon, the Genovian beach

Yeah. The beach. That's how far I had to drag Lilly to keep the entire palace from hearing her screaming at me.

Why me? Really? Why do I even hang out with her? I mean, she's fun to be around when she isn't being like THIS.

But THIS is just ridiculous. She's STILL yelling about how I have no right to tell her that she is incapable of finding love when I know perfectly well that she and Boris Pelkowski went out for nearly a year.

Um, yeah, before she DUMPED him for another man.

Although I am not about to point this out to her. As if I could even get a word in edgeways.

But if I could I'd remind her that it's not like I'm exactly thrilled with her gift for me either. Contrary to what Lilly may think, I do NOT need to learn 'how to express my ideas and stand up for myself' in my relationships, the way the title of the book she got me – *The Assertive Woman* – swears it will teach me. I am totally assertive. I pulled her out of the palace and made her come down here so she could go on screaming without disturbing anyone, didn't I?

Good thing I picked the beach too. This place is deserted. Possibly because it's only like fifty degrees and totally cloudy out. Also because, um, it's Christmas. Everyone – except for us – is at home having a nice time with their family members, probably doing that dumb olive-tree-branch thingy, or at least watching *A Christmas Story*, but whatever. Even the cruise ship is getting ready to go. There's only one other boat – one of the ones that carries tourists from the cruise ship over to the shore – bobbing around out there in the bay, with just a few people in it.

Still, I bet they can hear Lilly's screaming when the wind blows the right way.

'Why don't you just admit it?' she's shrieking. 'You're jealous of the fact that while you have had only one boyfriend in your entire life, in the past twenty-four hours I've had THREE!'

'Three?' I seriously cannot believe this. 'You're counting *Pierre*? Lilly, he's TWELVE.'

'Thirteen!' Lilly looks furious. 'And what's so wrong with a younger man adoring me? If it's good enough for Demi and Cameron, shouldn't it be good enough for me?'

'Lilly.' Really I don't know why I put up with her sometimes. 'That's not the point.'

'No, it isn't,' Lilly yells. 'Why don't we just admit the truth? You don't approve of my relationships with Lord Mulberry and Pierre because they're royals and I'm not, and you don't approve

239

of my relationship with Franco because he's a servant! You are such a PRINCESS!'

I am trying to be the voice of calm in the storm of passionate vitriol she is hurling at me, but it isn't easy when I feel so much like turning around and going back up to the palace. After all, that's where Michael is. Right now, instead of sitting on this knobby piece of driftwood writing this, I could be in Michael's arms. Well, if my dad wasn't looking, anyway.

'That isn't true, Lilly,' I say in what I hope is a very assertive voice. 'I don't approve of your relationship with Lord Mulberry because he is pro-hunting, as you well know. Besides, where can it go? As soon as he finds out the truth about your anti-monarchist leanings, he's going to run from you like a startled fawn. And I don't approve of your relationship with Pierre because you're too old to be dating someone who is so young he can ride for free on the New

York subway. And I don't approve of your relationship with Franco because it got in the way of his doing his job and now, because of you, he has none.'

'Like I held a gun to his head and MADE him punch Lord Mulberry,' Lilly says scathingly.

'You have a quality about you, Lilly, that some men – and boys – find hard to resist.'

I don't WANT to say this, because it's kind of complimentary, and it isn't like I *want* to compliment Lilly right now. But it's true. It was the last thing the Comte de Brissac said to me as his parents were dragging him off to their Rolls. 'Your friend has a quality about her,' Pierre managed to choke out, as his father tried to stuff him into the back seat, 'that no man could help but find intoxicating. Please tell her I will always love her, though others may try to keep us apart!'

'Uh,' I'd replied. 'Whatever you say, dude.'

Still. There may be something to it. It would

explain a lot about Lilly's – er – *varied* romantic life.

Lilly, much to my chagrin, looks flattered.

'Do I?' she coos.

I seriously want to throw up on her.

'Apparently,' I say. 'To tell you the truth, *I* don't see it. Lilly, don't you feel the least bit guilty over what you did to Franco?'

'You mean over what Franco did for love of me?' Lilly looks starry-eyed. 'Don't worry about Franco, Mia. He'll be all right. He was only doing this footman gig until he can get the job he really wants anyway.'

'Which is?'

'Snowboard instructor in Zermatt.'

'Well,' I say. 'Now he's going to have plenty of opportunity to work on that particular dream of his, isn't he?'

Is it my imagination or are the people in that boat out there WAVING to us?

'Oh, that remark is just so like you.' Lilly's stopped looking starry-eyed. She looks REALLY mad now. 'Not the *real* you of course. But the snotty you, the one you become when you're in Genovia.'

'What?' Now I know Lilly's lost her mind. Clearly she left it somewhere over the ocean during that transatlantic flight. 'What are you *talking* about? I am *not* snotty.'

'You so are.' Lilly looks really peeved. 'When you're in Genovia, you are. Admit it, Mia. You are totally two-faced. In New York you act all shy and self-deprecating – you're the very definition of a teen suffering from chronic low self-esteem. But when you're in Genovia it's like you're a different person! You have no problem telling people – in particular your so-called best friend – how to act and what to wear—'

OK, now she's gone too far.

'For your information, Lilly, I don't particularly LIKE the fact that I have to tell you not to wear rude T-shirts in front of my grandmother, or that it's wrong of you to organize games of strip bowling during her party. You're the one with the IQ of 210. I would think you'd KNOW better. But apparently in cases like this it's your EMOTIONAL IQ that counts, and we both know you aren't exactly *gifted* in that arena, now, ARE YOU? So what choice do I have but to tell you what to do, since you apparently can't figure it out for yourself?'

Lilly flushes. But she isn't ready to give in.

'But back in New York,' she shoots back, 'you make fun of your grandmother for being so worried about clothes and parties. Back home you're more concerned about global warming and over-population than you are about whether or not people show up at the breakfast table in their pyjamas. Here it's like you lose yourself in all this unimportant stuff, like tree-lightings and Advent calendars—'

'That stuff isn't unimportant,' I interrupt her. 'Yeah, it's not as important as global warming, but it's *tradition*, Lilly. And tradition is important too. So is respect. And it's disrespectful to come to breakfast in your pyjamas when you're staying in someone's palace.'

But Lilly still isn't giving up.

'I'm not the only one you boss around over here,' she declares. 'You tell EVERYONE what to do. Franco and Antoine and that maid who brings you hot chocolate in the morning—'

'Because I'm their BOSS, Lilly,' I explain. 'What do you think being a princess *means*? I have to run an entire country someday. In order to do that I'll have to give orders sometimes. It's not like I don't say please and thank you and try to be polite about it. But that's what princesses *do*. We *rule*.'

For the first time Lilly looks a little ashamed of herself.

'Well,' she says. 'It's just . . . well, I'm not used to it. It's weird to see you all . . . *ruling*.'

'Michael doesn't seem to have a problem with it,' I point out.

'Michael thinks it's hot,' Lilly says, not without some disgust.

Whoa. Michael thinks it's hot when I boss people around? Maybe it's time I started bossing *him* around a little . . .

Oh my God. That boat, the one with all the people on it . . . it's getting *really* close to the shore. And the people in it are totally shouting at us. I can't really tell what they're saying. But they look kind of upset. Some of them are scooping handfuls of water out of the boat and back into the ocean because—

BECAUSE THEIR BOAT IS SINKING!

Friday, December 25, 2 p.m.
royal Genovian dining room

Good thing the chefs counted on fifty for lunch. There's plenty to go around.

Which is good, because the people from the cruise ship are REALLY hungry.

The way they're going at the lobster bisque you'd think they hadn't had any food in weeks when in reality – according to Patty and Bud from Oklahoma – they enjoyed a full breakfast buffet just a few hours ago.

But I guess being stranded can stimulate the appetite.

Especially when, you know, you've paid 154 bucks (fifty-four for the under-twelve set, according to Patty, who left her two kids back on board on account of the cost and the fact that they just wanted to watch *Christmas Country Bear Jamboree* on pay-per-view anyway) for the privilege of strolling down the historic streets of Genovia, enjoying its quaint shops and outdoor markets, only to find all the shops closed and the markets shut down due to it being Christmas.

And then, as if all that was not bad enough, to have your boat sink on its way back to the ship. As Daryl from Seattle keeps putting it, 'Bummer, man.'

This seems to pretty much sum up the feelings of Joan from New Paltz, New York. Not to mention Jessica and Mike from Goshen, Indiana, Ann and Rick from Ann Arbor, Michigan, and even Chris and Jake from San Francisco.

But things are definitely looking up – all the passengers keep assuring us – now that they've got to see some real live royals . . . not to mention eat with them, and use some royal Genovian palace towels to dry themselves off.

I guess it would be putting it sort of mildly to

say Grandmere was surprised when Lilly and I came back from the beach with the Cruise Ship People in tow. When we first walked into the Great Hall, where everyone was still unwrapping gifts, she took one look at the group behind us – shivering in their sweatpants and Tevas – and pressed her lips together so hard they disappeared. Lilly later said she heard Grandmere mutter, 'First cats. Now Americans. What will she drag home next?'

But then her natural instincts as a hostess took over and Grandmere sent Antoine off for towels, hot tea and changes of clothes for our Christmas guests.

My dad wasn't nearly as sanguine about the whole thing. He immediately got on the phone and demanded to know why the cruise line hadn't come out to rescue their own passengers . . . not to mention where the Royal Genovian Coast Guard had been, leaving his

just parties and clothes and bossing people around. There's also making people feel welcome and at home, and saving them from potentially drowning in two feet of water.

I hope she realizes that guests have an obligation too, and that's to be polite and not get members of the household staff fired for hitting princes.

But this might be too much to hope for, even at Christmas time.

Patty says it's always been her dream to meet a real princess, so I posed for a picture with her and Bud, which Antoine said he'd be sure to mail to them, as soon as it's developed, since their own camera (fortunately one of those disposable ones) got soaked down on the beach.

Then Patty announced that her other dream had always been to meet a queen. By that she meant Grandmere, and not Queen Elizabeth (who left by royal helicopter last night just minutes after the fracas with her relation broke out). I tried explaining that Genovia is a principality, not a monarchy, and that Grandmere is Dowager Princess and not a queen. But Patty said she didn't care.

Instead she got up from the table, marched down to where Grandmere was sitting, staring in horrified fascination at Bud's mullet, and asked, 'Your Majesty, can I have your autograph?'

I was worried for a second that Grandmere might say no. But at the last minute she seemed to give in and went, 'Yes.'

Then she scrawled her name in Patty's scrapbook – which, Patty told me, she takes everywhere, because you never know when you might run into a moment you need to record for posterity. She's already pressed a bud from one of the bougainvillea plants outside on to her new 'Genovia' page, along with a tissue from the

Kleenex box in the guest bathroom and a tuft of Rommel's fur that went floating by in the air.

I guess this caught Grandmere's eye, since she started flipping through the book, going, 'And what is this?'

'Oh,' Patty said, looking modest. 'That's just my scrapbook.'

'Your what?' Tante Jean-Marie asked.

'My scrapbook,' Patty said. And then, when she saw the three royal sisters looking blank, she laughed and said, 'Don't y'all know what a scrapbook is? Why, I belong to three scrapbooking clubs: Rather B Scrappin', Scrap It and Scrappy Scrappers. We get together two, three times a month – sometimes more – to scrapbook.'

When Grandmere continued to look blank, Patty elaborated, 'To press our precious memories into books so that we'll always have a timeline of events to show our children and grandchildren.'

'Yeah, Grandmere,' I said, embarrassed that my own grandmother did not know of this timeless American pastime. Even though, of course, my own mother is so violently anti-scrapbook that she took the one someone gave her when Rocky was born and hammered it shut with nails and barbed wire, so now no one can open it. 'How come you don't keep a scrapbook?'

Grandmere gave me the evil eye.

'Princesses,' she said regally, 'don't scrapbook.'

'Well, that's a shame,' Patty said. 'It's very relaxing. And if you don't mind me saying so, Your Majesty, you look like you could use some relaxing.'

Grandmere looked extremely offended at this. But Patty didn't notice. She flipped open her scrapbook and started showing Grandmere all the different places she and Bud and the kids

any of Grandmere's guests had said to her all day. At least judging by the way Grandmere smiled.

Friday, December 25, 4 p.m., royal Genovian Great Hall

I can't believe we're STILL here, unwrapping presents. There are SO MANY.

At least the Cruise Ship People got off safely. The *Princess of the Seas* sent another motor launch for them.

Our goodbyes were almost tearful as we stood with our guests by the limos that were in the palace driveway, waiting to take them down to the dock. Chris and Jake promised to write. Olivia fussed over the Madame Alexander doll of me that I'd given her. Patty promised she'd send us each a little mini-scrapbook of their two-hour stay in the palace, so long as Antoine followed through on his promise to send her the photos he'd taken.

Since that's Antoine's job, I assured Patty that he would.

So after giving the Cruise Ship People a large hamper of food for their twenty-minute sea voyage – not to mention many of the other gifts we'd received and didn't want, such as the Dolce and Gabbana leg warmers Philomena got for me (good thing she is still in bed with that migraine), which Chris and Jake declared were totally fabulous, and Lilly's book for me on being assertive for Ann and my book for Lilly on finding the perfect man (we both agreed we don't actually need them any more) for Joan – we walked them to the waiting limos, where Patty turned and said, with tears in her eyes:

'We just can't thank y'all enough for your generosity. If everyone in Europe is as nice as y'all, the rest of our trip is going to be super.' Then, to Grandmere, she added, 'I'll put your official Rather B Scrappin' membership kit, along with a Gettin' Started handbook, in the mail just as soon as I get home, Your Majesty. You're just going to LOVE scrapbooking. I know it.'

Then they all got into the limos, and the chauffeurs drove them away, towards the docks and their waiting launch.

And I turned to Lilly and said, 'SEE?'

And she said, 'What?' all defensively.

And I said, 'THAT is what it means to be a princess.'

Lilly just sniffed and flounced back inside. As we followed her, Michael said softly to me, 'Actually I think that's what it means to be human, but no big deal.'

Which of course he's right about. But I'm glad Lilly didn't overhear him just the same.

And then we went inside to unwrap more presents.

Still, I'm almost sure Lilly gets it now. She is being much more polite to everyone, and even let Rommel have some of her *bûche de Noël*.

Ooooh, there are only two presents left under the tree . . . one giant one (mine for Michael) and a medium-sized one (his for me). Grandmere just had Antoine hand them to us, and said in a tired voice (and who can blame her? After all, she's been through quite a lot in the past twenty-four hours), 'Open them, please, so we can all go upstairs and nap until dinner.'

But Michael, to my utter delight and astonishment, went, 'Actually, Your Highness, would it be all right if Mia and I opened our presents for one another in private?'

And Grandmere looked relieved and said, 'Mazel tov,' and headed straight for the Sidecar Antoine had waiting for her on a silver tray.

So I guess we are going to open our presents in private!!!!

What could he have got me that he doesn't want everyone else to see????

Friday, December 25, 6 p.m., royal Genovian bedchamber

Oh my God! Michael is the best boyfriend EVER. **EVER.**

We totally took our presents out to the garden, where the royal gardeners had finally got rid of the last of the cats by putting bowls of vinegar around all of the flowerbeds (cats don't like the smell and stay away from areas the odour permeates. We discovered this when Fat Louie was a kitten and he decided to take revenge, peeing behind the futon every time I went to Genovia. We kept bowls of vinegar there for a while and he totally stopped).

So it kind of smelt less like bougainvillea out there in the royal garden and more like salad dressing.

But that was OK. Because nothing could ruin such a romantic moment. The sun even came out from behind the clouds while we were there, making rainbows in the jets from all the fountains, and down in the village the church bells started to ring for five o'clock Mass, and out in the harbour the *Princess of the Seas* tooted its farewell as it chugged off to Livorno, so it was way meaningful and all.

I told Michael to go first, so he pulled the wrapping paper off the poster I'd got him while I sat there on the edge of the fountain, anticipating his great delight over the extremely thoughtful and rare gift that I'd laboured so hard to get for him, and thinking about the huge French kiss it was likely to earn me.

But instead of delight suffusing his face when he saw Luke and Leia, confusion spread over it. Then he looked at me and went, 'Where did you get this?'

I just laughed at my own ingenuity and said,

'eBay! It's an original single-sided movie poster from 1977—'

'—in near mint condition,' Michael finished for me. Somewhat to my surprise. Because how had he known what I was going to say? Unless—

'Michael.' I felt a little sick to my stomach all of a sudden. And not because of all the *bûche de Noël* I'd ingested. 'You don't . . . I mean, how could you already have one of these? I never saw it on your wall—'

'Because I won it off a *Star Wars* fan site last month,' Michael said, starting to look amused about something. 'I figured I could sell it and make enough to get you something you'd really like for Christmas.'

I stared down at the poster, totally confused.

'But Michael,' I said. 'This can't be the same poster. Because you were here when I won the auction. And if you were here . . . who sent it to me?'

'My dad. I asked him to take care of it.'

'Your *dad*?' I couldn't believe it. 'But . . . didn't he notice when the shipping address was the Genovian palace?'

'Dad's not real detail-orientated,' Michael said, laughing now. 'I can't believe you were the one who bought my poster!'

I glared down at it. It didn't look nearly as nice as it had when I'd been wrapping it. Now it looked as if Princess Leia was kind of sneering at me. I couldn't believe it. First Dance Dance Party Revolution. Now this. Why could I never think of a decent gift to give my boyfriend?

'I'll sell it myself,' I said, reaching out to grab the poster from him. 'And buy you something really cool instead, something you'll really like.'

'No way,' Michael said, snatching the poster back. 'This *is* really cool, and I *do* really like it.'

'But.' I felt terrible. 'I got you something you already had!'

'Yeah,' Michael said, still grinning. 'And wanted to keep. And now I get to.'

Then he set the poster aside and held out his gift for me. 'Now you open yours.'

Still feeling terrible, I undid the silver ribbon on the package he set in my lap. I am such a loser, I was thinking. Out of all the sellers on eBay, how had I managed to buy something for Michael *from* Michael? Why hadn't the Madame Alexander doll company made the doll of me waving a banner that says *Loser* instead of *Save the Whales*? Because that would have been more appropriate.

Then I opened the box containing Michael's present to me and gasped.

Because inside it was Military Xander, the one *Buffy the Vampire Slayer* action figure I'd been missing.

'Oh, Michael,' I cried when I could finally speak. 'It's just perfect!'

'Really?' He grinned. 'I was hoping you'd like

it. It's the only one you don't have, right?'

And then, as if someone had kicked me, I remembered.

I must have gone pale or something, since Michael's grin faded and he looked at me with a suddenly worried expression.

'Mia?' he asked. 'Are you all right?'

'Oh, Michael,' I managed to choke out, feeling sicker to my stomach than ever.

I didn't want to tell him of course.

But what if he came over and saw the gap on my window sill where Giles had once stood?

'I don't have the complete collection any more,' I said miserably. 'I . . . I sold Fiesta Giles so I'd be able to afford the poster for you.'

The corners of Michael's lips twitched.

'You're kidding me, right?' he asked.

I shook my head. 'I wish I were.'

Michael made a noise. When I looked up, I saw – to my surprise – that he was laughing.

'Michael,' I said bewilderedly. 'Why are you laughing?'

'Why aren't you?' he wanted to know.

'Because this is your first Christmas in Genovia,' I said. 'And I wanted it to be really special. And instead everything's gone wrong! I thought at least I could get you a really great gift, but I couldn't even do *that* right.'

'Well, I don't have a whole lot of experience with them – Christmas presents, I mean,' Michael said, a little more seriously. 'But I have to say, this one is pretty special. The best Christmas present I ever had as a matter of fact.'

'But how can it be?' I felt more and more miserable every time I looked at that stupid poster. 'The best present you ever had, I mean? You obviously didn't want it in the first place if you *sold* it.'

'Are you kidding?' Michael asked, pulling me into his arms. 'The last thing I wanted to do was sell it. The only reason I did was to get enough money for something special for you.'

'Well,' I said, cupping a protective hand over Military Xander in case he was thinking of taking it away, like I'd tried to do with his poster, 'the only reason I sold Fiesta Giles was to get something special for you.'

'Well,' Michael said with another laugh. 'Then we're even. And I love my poster even more now *because* you got it for me.'

Really, what could I do after that except kiss him?

It was a very long time after that that Michael raised his head and said, 'Although the sight of your grandmother's face when she looked out into this garden and saw all of those cats? That was a pretty good present too.'

To which the only rational reply was, 'Michael, shut up and kiss me some more.'

And so he did.

The PRINCESS DIARIES
Princess Club

HEY, PRINCESS,
WANNA JOIN THE PRINCESS DIARIES PRINCESS CLUB?

4 fantastic comps and regular doses of fashion, gossip and games direct 2 ur mobile txt ur date of birth (dd,mm,yy)

to **07950 080700**

You will also get FREE unpublished snippets, exclusive games & comps!

08,11,91

The
PRINCESS
DIARIES

Guide to Life

Discover your inner princess!

If you've ever felt that deep down you're a princess, let Princess Mia and her very special guests guide you through life as a royal.

Includes fashion and beauty tips fit for a princess, plus advice on how to find your perfect prince.

The
PRINCESS
DIARIES

Princess Files

Princesses rule!

As a princess you will encounter plenty of problems and dilemmas. What do you do if an evil emperor threatens your planet? How do you avoid pricking your finger on a spindle? Fear not! Princess Mia and her friends are on hand to reveal how other princesses – past, present and pretend – can help you rule your life.

If Princess Leia and Cleopatra can overcome the baddies and find their one-true-loves, you can too – without kissing a single frog!

A selected list of titles available from Macmillan Children's Books

The prices shown below are correct at the time of going to press. However, Macmillan Publishers reserves the right to show new retail prices on covers which may differ from those previously advertised.

THE PRINCESS DIARIES Guide to Life	0 330 41539 5	£4.99
THE PRINCESS DIARIES Princess Files	0 330 42629 X	£4.99

All Pan Macmillan titles can be ordered from our website, www.panmacmillan.com, or from your local bookshop and are also available by post from:

Bookpost, PO Box 29, Douglas, Isle of Man IM99 1BQ
Credit cards accepted. For details:
Telephone: 01624 677237
Fax: 01624 670923
Email: bookshop@enterprise.net
www.bookpost.co.uk

Free postage and packing in the United Kingdom